Managing Voluntary Organisati

Other titles in the Charities Management series:

Rethinking Charity Trusteeship
Paul Palmer and Jenny Harrow

Managing Charitable Investments
John Harrison

Financial Management for Charities and Voluntary Organisations
Keith Manley

Meeting Need: Successful charity marketing
Ian Bruce

Foundations for Fundraising
Redmond Mullin

Charities and Taxation
Adrian Randall and Stephen Williams

Performance Measurement in Charities
David Wise

Managing Voluntary Organisations
New Approaches

Roger Courtney

ICSA Publishing
*The Official Publishing Company of
The Institute of Chartered Secretaries and
Administrators*

First published 1996 by
ICSA Publishing Limited
Campus 400, Maylands Avenue
Hemel Hempstead
Hertfordshire HP2 7EZ

© ICSA Publishing Ltd 1996

All rights reserved. No part of this publication may be reproduced, stored in a retrieval system, or transmitted, in any form, or by any means, electronic, mechanical, photocopying, recording or otherwise, without prior permission, in writing, from the publisher.

Typeset in 10/12½pt Palatino
by Hands Fotoset, Leicester

Printed and bound in Great Britain by
Redwood Books, Trowbridge, Wiltshire

British Library Cataloguing in Publication Data

A catalogue record for this book is available from the British Library

ISBN 1-87-2860-89-3

1 2 3 4 5   00 99 98 97 96

Contents

	Series editor's foreword	ix
	Preface	xi
	Acknowledgements	xiv
1	**Introduction**	1
	Chapter summary	1
	The voluntary sector and change	1
	Key themes	6
	Strategic planning and management	7
	Quality	7
	Training and development	8
	Identity of the voluntary sector	11
	Conclusion	16
	Key points	16
2	**Strategic planning and management**	18
	Chapter summary	18
	Blockages	19
	Benefits	20
	Strategic issues	23
	Main strategic options	25
	Where are we now?	25
	Dreaming	27
	Values	30
	Culture	32
	Policies	32
	External factors	36

Internal factors 40
Portfolio analysis 41
Long-term aims 44
Measures of success 48
Objectives 51
Plans and programmes 53
Resources 54
Monitoring 58
Commitment 60
Key points 63

3 Performance management 64

Chapter summary 64
Making plans effective 64
What is performance management? 64
Aims of performance management 66
Advantages for the individual 67
Advantages for the organisation 68
Implementation 68
Performance reviews 68
Common problems 69
Good practice 69
Key points 73

4 Quality assurance and management 74

Chapter summary 74
Quality of service 74
Definition 75
Standards 79
Moments of truth 79
Internal customers 84
Organisational model 85
Quality assurance 86
Quality systems 87
Quality problems 89
External recognition 89
Quality costs 96
Continuous improvement 97

	Creating a quality culture	98
	Assessment	99
	Key points	100
5	**Quality people**	**102**
	Chapter summary	102
	Competency approach	102
	National competency frameworks	104
	Relevant national standards	105
	Structure of national standards	106
	Uses	111
	Sharpening the saw: developing staff	112
	Investors in people	113
	Key points	119
6	**Quality managers**	**120**
	Chapter summary	120
	Work roles	122
	Personal effectiveness model	128
	Senior managers	129
	Uses of the management standards	131
	Evaluation	132
	Key points	134
7	**Putting it all together**	**135**
	Chapter summary	135
	Initiatives	135
	Key themes	136
	Where to start?	138
	Key points	140
8	**Two case studies**	**141**
	Major case study 1	141
	Major case study 2	146
Appendix 1	UK Quality Award – Learning from the success of others	153

Appendix 2	Management standards	157
Appendix 3	Personal competence model	159
References		160
Suggested further reading		164
Index		169

Series editor's foreword

Roger Courtney's depiction of charity management existing in an environment of constant 'white water' sets the pro-active approach of this book, the eighth in the series. For those who still believe that the charity sector is a quiet backwater requiring a suitable historic style of management, this book will come as something of a shock. Adapting the maxim that 'attack is the best form of defence', Courtney outlines and develops a series of management techniques which he explores within a framework of the external environment which charities now have to operate in. An environment that is not charitable.

With useful checklists and an approach to the quality management debate that is highly relevant to charities, this book provides charity managers a proforma to assess their own performance and their contribution to their charity's work. The book, however, goes beyond suggesting the adaptation of commercial strategies and prescriptive opinion. Courtney is someone who has had extensive and many years' experience as a charity manager. He provides practical illustrations and suggestions from the perspective of someone who understands the specific needs of the voluntary sector.

In previous forewords I have written of the lack of a recognised body of British literature on the sector. Some of the most popular books on the sector have been adoptions of best selling books written primarily for the private sector. While contributing to a literature, these books come from a perspective that has been reflected in many training courses for the voluntary sector. Essentially the voluntary sector is a receptacle for other sectors' management imports. While we can always learn from other sectors' experiences, the voluntary sector has its own unique characteristics. Many management practices pioneered by the voluntary sector have been adapted by the private and public sectors. Courtney's book is a further illustration that the voluntary sector has, and continues to develop, practices that are unique and exportable. The 'deficit balance' is starting to be addressed!

Dr Paul Palmer
Moores Rowland Director
Centre for Charity and Trust Research
South Bank University

Preface

Although there is no entirely accurate source of information on the size of the voluntary sector, the indications are that in Britain it now employs around a million people and has an income of almost £10 Million (Saxon-Harrold and Kendall 1995). According to the Charity Commissioners, in December 1994 there were 178,609 registered charities in England and Wales. However, this figure does not include the very large number of voluntary organisations who do not register (usually smaller groups) or cannot, because they do not comply with the ancient charity law requirements.

It has been estimated that the number of voluntary organisations has been expanding by around 2% each year (Bruce and Raymer 1992).

It is clear that the voluntary sector is a large and growing part of our national life. However, defining what exactly a voluntary organisation is, is by no means an easy task. Many of them benefit from the tax benefits of charitable status while others do not. Prince Philip in the 1994 Arnold Goodman lecture and Barry Knight in the 1993 Centris report re-opened the complex debate about the nature of the voluntary sector, the meaning of the word 'charity' and, which voluntary organisations should gain what tax benefits for their activities.

The voluntary sector (if indeed it is a sector at all – some would argue that it is part of the 'independent sector' along with the private sector) is also by no means a homogeneous group of organisations. It includes, for example, around 50 very large National organisations with turnovers in excess of £10M. The largest 200 charities each employ on average 500 staff, use 5,000 volunteers and have an income in excess of £1.3M. However only 11% of voluntary organisations have an income over £100,000

(Saxon-Harrold and Kendall 1995). The vast bulk of voluntary organisations are very small indeed, concentrating on one local area with a small number of volunteers and paid staff (if any). The precise number of such groups which are currently active, is unknown. There is also a large and diverse array of voluntary organisations falling somewhere between these two extremes.

Box 1

What are voluntary organisations?

According to Charles Handy "Voluntary organisations fall into five categories – with a lot of overlap.

There are the service providers, be they Scope, Dr Barnardo's, the National Trust or the Lifeboat Institution. Some of those will have over 1,000 paid staff and depend as much on government grants as on voluntary contributions for their existence.

There are those concerned with research and advocacy, ranging from the Child Poverty Action Group to the Campaign for Nuclear Disarmament to radical action groups in local communities or specialist journals.

Then there are the self-help groups that give support and assistance, to single parents, for example, or to those caring for sufferers from disease, or the groups which have sprung up to support the unemployed.

There is also another form of self-help group, that of those who share a common interest or enthusiasm, be it for playing cricket, gardening or kite-flying. The clubs and societies for leisure interests don't think of themselves as voluntary organisations or as volunteers but they are there from choice not for pay and there are lots of them, an important part of our society.

Lastly there are the intermediary bodies, like the councils for voluntary service, which are there to provide help with skills and advice on policy.

Many will fall into more than one category. Shelter, for example, is both a campaigning organisation for better housing and a provider of accommodation and advice to the homeless.

No wonder the scene is confusing to the outsider when such a wide variety consorts under the same umbrella name."

Handy 1988 – from 'Understanding voluntary organisations.'

(See Box 1 for one view of the different types of voluntary organisations.)

Despite its size and the scope of its work the voluntary sector still faces problems in how it is perceived by the public, who generally view voluntary organisations as amateur, run by well-meaning, committed people 'insulated from the pressures and realities of the Modern age' (Hinton 1993), and certainly not as the complex, dynamic, pressured operations that many of them are.

To illustrate this attitude, Nicholas Hinton, then Director General of The Save the Children Fund, with a turnover in excess of £100M, tells the story of being at a cocktail party and on being asked what he does, replies that he is Director General of Save the Children. To which the questioner responds 'That must be very worthwhile – is it full-time?' (Bruce 1993).

The story typifies a very traditional attitude towards charities. However, as more and more is demanded of the voluntary sector, so both the practice and perception of voluntary organisations are starting to change.

The management of voluntary organisations is becoming more and more sophisticated requiring an increasing level of skills in its Trustees, staff and volunteers. Those involved in, or in contact with, these voluntary organisations are also becoming more aware of this growing professionalism and the need for even greater professionalism in future.

The fundamental purpose of this book is to look at some of the changes currently taking place in the UK which are having an impact on the *management* of voluntary organisations and to highlight the steps which some organisations are taking to respond to and, in some cases pre-empt, these changes and thereby become more successful in achieving their aims.

Acknowledgements

I would like to thank the following who read early versions of this book and provided helpful comments: Dr Brendon Murtagh, Quintin Oliver, Dr Arthur Williamson, Dr Paul Palmer, Brian Courtney and Christine Woods; to the staff, volunteers and residents of the Simon Community (Northern Ireland) for bringing much needed reality to bear on the developing theories and ideas that are explored in the book; and most of all, to Christine, Emma and Carol for their forebearance while it was being written.

1 Introduction

Chapter summary

The environment in which voluntary organisations operate is going through a period of substantial and rapid change that is having an enormous impact on the voluntary sector as a whole and on individual organisations. In order to respond to the many challenges that voluntary organisations face, there is a need to develop more effective strategies for their management. Some of the key initiatives that have been developed by voluntary organisations include: strategic planning and management; performance management; quality assurance and management; competence-based recruitment and development; and Investors in people. Although coming from different sources and using different terminology these initiatives can be developed within an integrated model to help voluntary organisations achieve their goals much more effectively.

The voluntary sector and change

The voluntary sector, by its very nature, is about change. That's why people join it. They want to help individuals and communities to improve the quality of their lives, sometimes by providing services, sometimes by campaigning to change laws or policies that affect these individuals or communities.

However, particularly to those inside it, the voluntary sector can, at times, seem to be far from being in control of change, but instead appears to be being buffeted by a whirlwind of external factors which are having an enormous impact on it. It can be argued that voluntary organisations which fail to take account of

> **Box 1.1**
>
> **What is the voluntary sector?**
>
> In the 12th Arnold Goodman Charity Lecture, in 1995, the Viscount Whitelaw summarised his view of the voluntary sector as follows:
>
> Here is a wild garden, a rampant display of plants of all shapes and sizes, some hugging the ground, others dominating the landscape. Here is a vast array of organisations occupied with every conceivable human activity – mostly small, but some huge; merging at one end of the spectrum into the private world of the family, then emerging into the neighbourhood and ending as players on the world stage.
>
> The sector's most fundamental contribution is in providing a point of contact between the public and the private, in enabling private action for the public good. Charities – voluntary organisations – are the means by which free individuals collectively express their commitment to something beyond their private selves.
>
> It is through charities and other voluntary organisations that we lay claim, as free individuals, to the right effectively to act in the public arena and to change for the better the condition of our fellow citizens. In a vital way, you might say that charities 'set the tone' for the society of which they are a part.
>
> Whitelaw 1995

these changes, at best will not achieve their aims, and at worst may not be around very long. The way in which the voluntary sector as a whole responds to them is also crucial to the future of the sector.

To set out my own stall, I believe there is something enormously powerful, motivating and distinctive about the voluntary sector, which I want to see both preserved and promoted. As Tony Blair MP has said:

> As an instrument of public intervention, voluntary organisations have proved themselves time and time again to be highly creative, efficient and unfailing in tackling the problems in our society, improving the quality of life for many and in serving others (Blair 1994).

In the midst of a wide range of quite fundamental external changes I don't believe that the best way to preserve and promote the voluntary sector will be to simply try to minimise the impact of these changes, keep our heads down and do things the way we have always done them in the past. I believe we fundamentally need to transform the way voluntary organisations are managed to meet these challenges head on.

So, what are these external changes that are sweeping over the voluntary sector?

1. Government has substantially altered the boundaries of the public sector. More and more chunks of government, and areas that used to be considered the domain of public sector services are being pushed into the so-called 'Independent' sector; some into profit-making ventures, others into the voluntary sector and some into a shadowy quagmire which lies somewhere in between all three main sectors (for example Housing Associations and Health and Social Services Trusts).

    This means that there is significant growth taking place in the voluntary sector as new organisations take to the field and compete for very limited resources. This reinforces the need for increased professionalism in fund raising and other aspects of income generation as well as in other aspects of management and marketing.

    This change also confronts a traditional perception of the voluntary sector which particularly developed in the 1960s and 70s, in the field of Social Services. This viewed the primary role of the voluntary sector as to be pioneering and to undertake exciting innovative work, which if successful would be taken over by Government as mainstream public programmes. With a few notable exceptions those days, if they ever existed, would appear to be long gone. The provision of mainstream services is seen increasingly as the role of both for profit and non-profit agencies.

2. There is the related move from the grant aid of voluntary organisations to the purchasing or contracting of specific services. Fast disappearing are the days when an organisation received an annual block grant which, as long as the government body felt the organisation was doing 'a good job', would continue to be received in order for the organisation to be able to keep doing 'the good job', whatever that might be. Today, organisations are increasingly likely to

be tendering to statutory purchasing agencies for contracts to carry out pieces of defined work to specified standards. In this process voluntary organisations are as likely to be competing against private sector or indeed public sector providers as other voluntary agencies. In this situation if the organisation doesn't win the contract for a particular period because it doesn't meet the standards or someone else is cheaper, then they don't get the work, or the money, and for some voluntary organisations this has already meant closing their doors.

3. Linked to the previous two points, is the impact of the Government's 'scrutiny report' which, as well as forcing government departments and agencies to develop more coherent policies in relation to support for the voluntary sector, also means a much higher level of accountability in relation to this support, including three-yearly external evaluations of voluntary organisations receiving funds. These evaluations are often the catalyst for quite fundamental changes in an organisation.

4. The Charities Act in Britain, and the new statement of recommended practice in charity accounting (SORP II) reflect the demand for greater public accountability, so that general donors can see where and how their money is spent and feel confident that there is effective protection against abuse. There have been a number of well publicised and some lesser-publicised cases of such abuse in the voluntary sector recently. Such problems have the potential to do enormous damage both to individual organisations and the sector as a whole.

5. What is sometimes called the social care (or 'human service') sector is facing a range of additional changes.

    (a) The Care in the Community Initiative reflected the widely held view that individuals in need should be cared for 'in the community' rather than in hospitals or other large institutions and has resulted in an explosion in public, private and voluntary sector community-based facilities and the run-down of many larger usually public sector facilities.

    (b) The Community Care Regulations in 1993 transformed the process and funding for individuals entering

community-based facilities and have already resulted in the closure of a number of these facilities.
(c) The Children Act in England and Wales (and the equivalent new Children legislation in Scotland and Northern Ireland) attempts to redress the balance in policy and practice towards the needs and aspirations of children themselves.
(d) The fundamental restructuring of health and social services into individual community and hospital trusts has formalised the split between purchasers and providers of services. This has created some confusion both within the voluntary sector and the statutory sector. Having spent years getting used to dealing with various levels of social workers and principal social workers, the staff and volunteers of voluntary organisations now find that they are often dealing with the same individuals but now bearing titles like 'Business Development and Contracts Manager'!
6. The development of the European Union also creates an increasingly international dimension to the work of voluntary organisations with greater possibilities of partnerships across Europe, the gaining of European funding, and the influence of policy developments in the European union.

When all these changes (and there are undoubtedly many others which could have been mentioned, such as technological change) are looked at together it almost seems that the voluntary sector is being fundamentally transformed by a host of factors not of its making. Some people in the voluntary sector feel that they are just desperately struggling to keep up with the game. Some even feel that as soon as they think they are on top of what the game is then the rules are changed.

Ian Bruce has summarised the situation in the following terms:

The voluntary sector in general, and charities in particular, are now entering a major phase of change and growth.

Such a turbulent situation could be described as 'permanent white water' (Weisbord 1987). It can be argued that the voluntary sector has now emerged from a long voyage over the last 50 years down relatively well-charted waterways to face a 'tempest-lashed open sea'. This emphasises the need for organisations to be well-equipped to both prepare for and to create change.

Key themes

I believe that many of these changes, if dealt with in the wrong way, are indeed a threat to the voluntary sector, but they also create very important opportunities to develop a *more* effective voluntary sector, without losing its distinctive identity. However this will require a more positive pro-active approach.

Some of the key themes of this new approach are:

1. The need to be clearer about the purpose and values of the voluntary sector and of each individual voluntary organisation in an increasingly crowded market place.
2. The need for clearer visibility and accountability of funding to specific outcomes, standards and objectives.
3. The more efficient use of resources and greater visibility of this efficiency.
4. The continued expansion of the scope of the work that the voluntary sector is involved in, which will be increasingly in a very mixed and competitive environment of public, private and expanding voluntary sector providers.
5. An increasing development of partnerships between agencies, across sectors and countries.
6. Greater accountability to clients, users, or customers (the appropriate terminology for the beneficiaries of the services will be different for each individual organisation). The need to refocus continuously so that their aspirations and views are the centre of the work of the organisation will become increasingly important.
7. And, last, but by no means least, the skills of those required to work and manage in the voluntary sector (trustees, staff and volunteers) are changing rapidly. The need to develop and update these skills presents a major challenge if organisations are to manage the changes needed effectively.

So what are the new directions in the management of the voluntary sector going to need to be, in light of all this, if that management is to be effective and keep the special identity of the voluntary sector?

Strategic planning and management

The first major focus is strategic planning and management.

Only if organisations systematically look at themselves and the environment in which they operate on a regular basis, evaluate their own strengths and weaknesses, assess the external opportunities and threats that exist and clarify their own principles and priorities, can they be sure that they are doing the right things, the things they do best. A real danger in not having a clear set of aims and objectives, in the new contracting culture, is that organisations will let the funding tail wag the dog, simply putting in bids wherever they think the money is, rather than on the basis of their vision of what they would like to see changed, which is the very essence of the voluntary sector. Charles Handy calls this behaviour 'strategic delinquency' (Handy 1988) and argues that it can lead to 'strategic seduction' by the lure of money.

The very survival of an organisation can also be at risk without effective strategic planning. In *What a way to run a railroad* the authors analysed the reasons for the failure of many radical and progressive initiatives (particularly in the field of publishing) during the 1970s. One of the conclusions they came to was that:

> one crucial function of management . . . is the clarification of organisational goals and the continuous development and monitoring of strategies to achieve these goals. The problem of how to clarify objectives, create a strategy to carry them out and find the means to make them happen, is one that few radical organisations recognise explicitly. Most just muddle through. This lack of strategic clarity can only be a recipe for disaster, as the history of failure in this sector over the last few years plainly demonstrates. (Landry *et al* 1985)

J Steven Ott reviewing three non-profit management books for *Non-profit Management and Leadership* argues that because of the impact of the external environment and the complex multiple constituencies of stakeholders of voluntary organisations that:

> organisational mission and vision are more crucial for the success of non-profit organisations than for for-profits and government organisations. (Ott 1991)

Quality

The second major focus for voluntary sector management in

future will be on quality as defined by users, clients, customers and funders. I think voluntary organisations will be increasingly asking their users what standards of service they would hope for (not just a minimum) and drawing up detailed specifications and procedures to ensure that these are consistently met and indeed exceeded. These quality initiatives are likely to have four main elements:

1. The empowerment of users, clients, customers to ensure they have a much more effective voice in expressing their aspirations, and their complaints.
2. The establishment of quality teams throughout organisations which meet regularly to look at how to improve the way things are done. This is often called the total quality management (TQM) approach.
3. The establishment of quality assurance systems such as BS EN ISO 9000 to provide clear and straightforward procedures to meet the quality standards every time. Systems are also needed to ensure that each time the standards are not met there is action to ensure that the same problem does not recur.
4. And lastly, regular evaluations of services to ensure they are effective, efficient and equitable. Some agencies working with people who have mental health problems and those with learning difficulties, for example, have already developed some very interesting models which try to combine quality assurance and evaluation, primarily by the users. Such evaluations may in turn have major implications for strategy.

As Kearns *et al* argue in *Why non-profit organisations are ripe for total quality management* (1994)

The fundamental principles of Customer Satisfaction, problem prevention, employee empowerment, and quality management are, and always have been, the bedrock of effective management and organisational success. The systematic application of these principles in non-profit organisations should be a component of a long-term strategy for survival and growth.

Training and development

The third area that is crucial to the future of the voluntary sector is training and development. The external changes taking place are putting enormous strains on the traditional skills that exist in the voluntary sector. It is interesting to note that a recent survey of voluntary organisations in Britain showed that 53% of appointments to senior posts were made from outside the voluntary sector (Bruce 1992). That must be very disheartening for the unsuccessful candidates from the voluntary sector. It can also be seen as an indictment of the management training that is available to them.

We need a much greater emphasis on training in its broadest sense, not only to enable individual staff and volunteers to develop but to ensure that the kinds of aims and objectives that come out of the strategic planning discussed earlier are achieved *and* the continually improving quality standards that are expected are met.

To do this it is necessary to continually review the skills and knowledge that trustees, staff and volunteers require in order to achieve these goals and focus training on these key skills and knowledge.

There needs to be training at three main levels:

1. Trustees or management committee members. For better or worse these are key players in all voluntary organisations and it must be very difficult for them to play an effective role in light of a whirlwind of changes which they often don't understand on top of an already unclear and ambiguous role. It is sometimes only when the roof falls in that trustees realise the enormous responsibility that they have taken on.

    There is therefore a crucial need for greater training made available to trustees to enable them to do their job.

2. Managers in the voluntary sector. Some of the developing skills areas for managers in the voluntary sector are:
    - Strategic planning;
    - Financial management;
    - Negotiating contracts;
    - Quality assurance;
    - Income generation;
    - Evaluation;
    - Training and development.

    There are undoubtedly many others that a detailed training

needs analysis (TNA) across the sector would reveal. Indeed, a survey of charity chief executives in 1991/92 highlighted 'strategic planning', 'awareness of customer needs', 'financial control', 'raising income level', and 'concern for quality' as the most important charity managerial attributes for the future post-recession. (Bruce and Raymer 1992)

Although many managers come from outside the sector, probably most managers in the voluntary sector became managers because they were good at their non-managerial job and therefore by a sort of osmosis naturally moved up, often with little in the way of induction or training.

Management requires a wholly different range of skills from other jobs; some of those skills have already been mentioned. It can be argued that the level of training available to managers and those aspiring to management in the voluntary sector at present is very inadequate and needs to be urgently addressed (see Bruce and Leat 1993). The management charter initiative (MCI) gives us the opportunity to be much clearer about what we expect of managers and therefore the opportunity to develop a range of training options to meet their needs and those of the organisation, in this new world.

3. Voluntary sector staff and volunteers. The third important development in training is the establishment of National Vocational Qualifications (and Scottish Vocational Qualifications). Voluntary organisations are a major employer of individuals (both paid and unpaid) with a low level of educational attainment and often little in the way of accredited technical or professional training. The development of NVQs should provide the opportunity to ensure that all staff and volunteers can get proper accreditation for their substantial work-related skills and knowledge, if they want it, and a framework to develop new skills and knowledge through competence-based training. National competency standards can also be very useful in role clarification, recruitment and selection, appraisal and succession planning.

Hopefully, the voluntary sector will take on board these three training areas and also take the lead in the Investors in people initiative which helps organisations relate their strategic goals to the training and development needs of the individuals within the organisation. Investors in people has been generally slow to get off the ground in the voluntary sector but hopefully this can be quickly rectified.

Identity of the voluntary sector

Some of the key development areas in the management of voluntary organisations which will enable them to be more effective in achieving their visions of change are highlighted above. However there are some people in the voluntary sector who are highly critical of this whole approach to the development of the voluntary sector.

The criticism arises because in some cases the models and techniques suggested have been developed in industry and the language is sometimes borrowed from the private sector. The concern is sometimes expressed that the voluntary sector will loose its identity if it goes down this road and become indistinguishable from the private sector.

Diana Leat in *Managing Across Sectors* (1993) points out that:

Traditionally voluntary organisations have taken little interest in 'management'. Doing good has been seen as sufficient in itself and non-profit organisations have been reluctant to spend money on anything other than the immediate task. But lack of interest goes deeper than that.

'Management' may be not merely unnecessary but positively dangerous. Non-profit organisations may well point out that they have survived and, in many cases, thrived without the benefit of highly paid managers and fancy management theories. Organisations have feared that their goals will be deflected by 'professional' managers and management concepts and practices largely drawn from the for-profit sector. Many non-profit organisations do not accept the tendency to conflate 'businesslike' and 'efficient' with professional management and have yet to be convinced that management concepts and techniques derived from the for-profit sector are the best or the only ones available.

Charles Handy (1988) reinforces this point (see Box 1.2) which he attributes to 'ideological fanaticism'. I think this is an important issue not to be dodged and there are a number of comments that need to be made in response.

If one looks at the development of both private sector and public sector organisations it can be seen that many of them are

> **Box 1.2**
>
> **Ideological fanaticism**
>
> At times the rejection of management and all it stands for goes to extremes. Those who came of age in 1968 and moved into the world of alternative organisations in the 1970s developed a new set of bad words:
>
> - 'Success': to be successful was to risk contamination and to compromise your principles. It was better to stay pure and fail; indeed, perhaps the only way to stay pure is to fail, to be a 'drabbie' rather than a 'yuppie'. Thus it was that many preferred to tilt against the windmills of society instead of building ones that worked better.
> - 'Structures': structures imply hierarchy, they suggest that one individual is entitled to more authority than another. Ironically, the lack of structures allowed informal power elites to arise, cabals to be created, deals to be fixed in private and organisations to become corrupted.
> - 'Professionalism': professions got a bad name in the 1970s, for creating dependence and for assuming incapacity in others. To believe should be enough, and so the voluntary world became the refuge of Britain's favoured species, the enthusiastic amateurs, whereas professionalism proper means doing things well.
> - 'Leadership': community was all, togetherness was what mattered; no one person should try to impose his or her views. Indeed, leadership is risky; it means exposing one self to rejection and to unpopularity. Leaderless groups, however, can become endless encounter groups more interested in discussing why than in doing it, which was the experience of many in the 1970s.
>
> From Handy 1988

starting to use a range of ideas and methods which are more commonplace in the voluntary sector. These include:

- the importance of a strong ethical value base;

- the idea of the empowerment of staff and customers;
- the value of small, flat and flexible organisations;
- teamwork;
- the involvement of all staff in decisions that affect them and the future of the organisation;
- customer care;
- the development of management and corporate responsibility;
- the importance of non-executive input at a strategic level;
- inter-agency collaborations.

Peter Drucker (1990) argues that the private and public sectors have a lot to learn from the voluntary sector. Indeed he argues that some of the best management is now found in non-profit organisations and that the business organisations of the future are more likely to resemble the best non-profit organisations of today than the historical manufacturing company of the past. It is not all one way traffic.

Diana Leat (1993) herself argues that:

If 'best management' is equated with the principles laid down in such popular texts as Peters and Waterman's *In Search of Excellence* then non-profits are worth a closer look.

Peters and Waterman (1982) suggest that eight attributes characterise 'excellent' American commercial companies. These are: a bias for action, staying close to the customer, autonomy and entrepreneurship, productivity through people, a hands-on and value-driven approach, sticking to the knitting, simple form and lean staff, and simultaneous loose-tight properties. These eight attributes might well be a description of the ideology, if not the practice, of many non-profit organisations.

First, many non-profit organisations display a bias for action – for getting on and doing things rather than talking or thinking about it. Secondly, non-profits emphasise their concern for the wishes and needs of their customers; this is what in many respects provides them with their *raison d'être*.

Thirdly, autonomy and entrepreneurship are an important part of the ideology of the non-profit sector which prides itself on being a source of innovation.

Fourthly, people are typically seen as the key resource of the non-profit organisation. Many have no other resource and even those with a substantial income are still likely to emphasise the importance of involving staff and volunteers in the work of the organisation. Fifthly, non-profits also stress the importance of a hands-on, value driven approach; values are at the core of the organisation's mission and hands-on knowledge and involvement are considered crucial. Sixthly, for various reasons, non-profits display a strong tendency to 'stick to the knitting' – so stay close to the business they know best. Seventhly, although it is debatable whether many non-profits could be described as displaying a simple form, they are likely to display lean staff. 'Lean staff' may be due to lack of income and/or because a large paid staff and high expenditure on 'administration' are frowned on as an unnecessary diversion of charitable resources.

Finally, many non-profits have simultaneous loose-tight structures, strongly emphasising core values but allowing workers considerable freedom within that. As noted above, the emphasis on core values stems from their centrality to mission and, for some, to charitable status.

To maintain the voluntary sector's identity it is also vital to maintain the sector's distinctive campaigning edge; to take up unpopular issues and to criticise government bodies when necessary. If the sector is going to have a expanding role in providing services and other activities with and for people who have specific needs it also has a responsibility to look at the bigger picture and demonstrate how the lives of their beneficiaries are affected by government decisions and policies and to try and change them.

This is also why strategic planning is so important. In light of the distinctive values and priorities of the voluntary sector individual organisations need to focus on those in greatest need who may well not be on the top of government's priority list and therefore more difficult to get resources for. If the voluntary sector is to maintain its integrity and distinctiveness it must not be sucked into merely reflecting government priorities but must do all in its power to work with and on behalf of those individuals, groups and communities who need an effective voluntary sector the most.

In using techniques and models that have been developed in the private sector it is important to ensure that the private sector view of other agencies in the same sector as competitors is not accepted. The voluntary sector has a strong and positive tradition of collaborating on issues of mutual concern and there are a large number of examples of agencies working together on particular projects or services as partners. This collaborative tradition needs to be strengthened and developed by an openness between voluntary organisations with similar objectives and a willingness to develop partnerships of various sorts.

Box 1.3

Richard Smith the Director of Support Centres of America, writing in *The Chronicle of Philanthropy* (May 1994) is particularly caustic about the suggestion that is sometimes made that voluntary organisations should behave more like private companies.

It always makes me nervous when I hear or read someone say or write 'we need to run charities like big business.' The reason for my trepidation is simple: I am never quite sure what the advocate of this general prescription is really suggesting.

Is it that non-profit organisations should emulate big business by making as much money as possible? or cutting ethical corners to accomplish company ends? or is it providing senior executives with ridiculous compensation packages? or how about sacrificing important social goals to achieve corporate goals or is it managing an organisation with skill and competence to maximise the accomplishment of the mission?

If it's the latter, why not just say it? We do not need to confuse the matter with sweeping generalisations about the similarities of non-profit and big-business practices. Lets just say what we really mean: Effective non-profit organisations are critical to the health and welfare of everyone in society and these non-profit managers and boards must be committed to the pursuit of excellent management and governance practices. In other words, the pursuit of excellence is as important in non-profit enterprise as it is in for-profit enterprise.

The tendency towards competition which is reinforced by the contract culture needs to be fought by the voluntary sector as a whole and by individual voluntary organisations showing that working together in partnership is in the long-term much more effective and efficient than dog-eat-dog competition.

Robert Herman in his article *Preparing for the future of non-profit management* (1994) argues that 'the virtues of co-operation and community are too-little valued, and in a society in which individualism, competition, and large-scale organisations operating on universalistic criteria leave people searching for meaning and connectedness, family, neighbourhood, church, and voluntary organisations have long been sources of social integration, personal meaning, and connectedness. All of these institutions are changing. As they change, will they continue to offer people the same opportunities to achieve social integration, meaning, and connectedness? Will they continue to be the foundations of community? More particularly, if it is true that greater competition is the likely trend for non-profit organisations, what can and should the leaders and managers of non-profit organisations do to counteract that trend?' (Herman 1994)

Conclusion

The voluntary sector is facing an exceptional period of change which will require an exceptional response from those responsible for and working in the voluntary sector.

In particular voluntary organisations will need to develop their skills in:

- Strategic planning and management;
- Performance management;
- Quality assurance and management;
- The training and development of its personnel (paid and unpaid).

In the following chapters each of the main themes outlined above is explored in greater depth. Each chapter is designed to be a guide to the relevant area, containing various practical tools and techniques which should in themselves help a voluntary organisation to develop in the pursuit of excellence. I believe however, that they are most powerful looked at as a whole, each chapter reinforcing the others. However, organisational change is a long-term process and every organisation will need a point of entry, which ideally should be strategic planning, other aspects of the process of development being planned over a number of years.

Organisational development is an exciting and enriching journey without end.

Key points

- The voluntary sector is in the midst of a period of enormous change which presents opportunities as well as threats to the sector and to individual organisations.

- To deal with the threats and take advantage of the opportunities the management of voluntary organisations is becoming increasingly professional.
- Strategic planning and management is crucial in giving voluntary organisations a clear and coherent focus to its work.
- Quality assurance and management enable voluntary organisations to consistently meet the agreed needs of their beneficiaries.
- A competence-based approach to staff selection and development enables organisations to ensure it has the right people with the right skills.

2 Strategic planning and management

> When we talk of tomorrow the Gods laugh
>
> Chinese proverb

Chapter summary

In an unstable environment strategic planning and management is particularly important in giving an organisation coherence and direction to its decisions and actions. This chapter develops a model of strategic planning and management appropriate to the needs of the voluntary sector. The model presented helps a voluntary organisation to analyse its external environment to identify trends which may present opportunities and/or threats and to look internally at its own strengths and weaknesses. On the basis of this analysis, organisations are taken through a process of development of a clear mission/vision statement, long-term aims, specific measurable objectives, and plans and programmes. The model presented enables progress to be measured against stated aims and objectives, monitored, and the resource implications to be assessed. Strategic planning and management does not necessarily mean that each phase of the model falls neatly after the previous one. Any of the phases may have important implications for the other phases, which may then need to be reviewed.

Voluntary organisations are sometimes accused of adopting a 'Christopher Columbus' approach to management: despite consulting all the available maps, when he left for the 'New World' he wasn't too sure what his destination would be; when he arrived he wasn't too sure where he was; and when he got home he didn't know where he had been!

This reinforces the point made by David Saint (1994) that 'Strategic planning is rather like sailing a ship, you work out where you are going, the vessel you will use, and the supplies you need to get there. You plot your course and estimate how long the journey will take.

Despite the fact that modern ideas of strategic planning and management have been around for more than thirty years (particularly since the writing of Ansoff in the 1960s) they are showing no sign of being a passing fad. Many voluntary organisations however (with some notable exceptions) have failed to take on board the need to develop coherent and relevant plans for the future and regularly monitor and revise these plans in light of changing circumstances. As a result they are often dogged by perpetual 'crisis management' or 'firefighting'. In a very real sense 'failing to plan is planning to fail'.

From a study of 103 non-profit organisations in the USA, Unterman and Davis conclude that:

Not only have not-for-profit organisations failed to reach the strategic management stage of development, but many of them have failed to reach even the strategic planning stages that for profit enterprises initiated 15–20 years ago. (Waterman and Davis 1982)

This is also arguably the case in the UK, although it is true that there are many for-profit companies as well where the level of strategic management is at a very low level, as there are some voluntary organisations who have set a high standard of strategic planning and management.

Blockages

It is not difficult to understand why most voluntary organisations do not do this kind of strategic planning and management (many small private companies are the same). They are often short of staff and resources, constantly working at a stretch even to do the day-to-day job that they feel they exist to do. Without the funding to carry out their current role properly it is hard to summon up the energy to develop new plans with no indication where the money might come from. The world around them is also changing so rapidly that once the ink on any plan would be dry it might be out of date. Creating a three- or five-year plan in these circumstances would seem almost an irrelevance. As a result many glossy plans seem to appear in a blaze of glory and then quietly disappear in the harsh glare of reality.

Some cynical individuals would argue that strategic planning is like mating elephants: it all happens in high places and takes a very long time to bear results, if it ever does. However as Christopher Spence, the director of London Lighthouse has pointed out:

for all its technicality, the strategic plan is simply the map which keeps us on track, guiding us through such a complex maze of change. (Spence 1994)

It could be argued that strategic planning and management is a particular skill that is not commonly found in the backgrounds of those who go to work (paid and unpaid) in the voluntary sector, because they tend to be individuals who are much more concerned about the urgent needs of people. It can also sound dangerously like something imported from the profit-focused private sector, (even the military in some cases) and therefore at best not something appropriate for the voluntary sector. The jargon used in strategic planning (see Box 2.1) tends to reinforce this negative image.

There is however another way of viewing it, not only as a valuable tool that the voluntary sector can use, but as an absolute necessity if voluntary organisations are going to survive and develop in an increasingly competitive and changing environment. This is borne out by recent research on the largest charities in the UK which has shown an 'increasing awareness of the importance of strategic planning' (Bruce 1993).

When a group of charity chief executives were asked in 1986/7 what were the most important charity managerial attributes 'strategic planning' came in sixth place. When the exercise was repeated in 1991/2 it had moved up to second place, but was given first place for attributes that would be required for the future post-recession.

Benefits

A strategic approach to planning and management has a range of potential benefits which include the following:

1. Opportunities are identified, evaluated and capitalised on.
2. Threats are identified, evaluated and avoided or where they can not be avoided the impact of them can be minimised. Contingency plans can be established for what to do in the event of a particular potential threat happening. Different scenarios can be explored, so an organisation can be prepared for different eventualities.
3. Internal strengths and unique selling points are identified and built on.
4. Internal weaknesses are identified, and corrected, compensated for or the impact of them minimised.
5. The purpose and direction of the organisation is clarified so everyone is pulling in the same direction.
6. The distinct culture/values/principles of the organisation (i.e.: 'the way we do things round here') is clarified and built on.
7. Clear, achievable objectives and standards are identified that people can work towards and know if they have been achieved.
8. Donors/funders can be given the opportunity to invest in the creation of a clear and positive vision of the future. They know what their funding will achieve.
9. Limited material and financial resources can be targeted on clear priorities.
10. The morale of trustees, staff and volunteers is likely to improve with clearer goals and achievements.
11. The human resource strategy of the organisation can be focused on achieving specific organisational goals.
12. Progress can be regularly and clearly monitored, because it is clear what the organisation is trying to achieve.

The strategic planning process can also be a very powerful tool for clarifying others' views of the organisation and developing partnerships both formal and informal with other bodies (statutory, private and voluntary).

Almost none of the above depends on the production of a long and glossy document called the strategic or development plan, or whatever. The benefits are the product of carrying out the process of planning. As Dwight D. Eisenhower said 'plans are nothing, planning is everything!'

Box 2.1

Jargon

One of the difficulties faced by any organisation deciding on the precise strategic planning and management process to use is that they realise on reading the relevant literature that everyone uses different terminology and there is no real consensus on the exact meaning of words such as:-

- Mission
- Vision
- Purpose
- Philosophy
- Values
- Principles
- Culture
- Goals
- Aims
- Targets
- Standards
- Objectives
- Sub-objectives
- Policies
- Programmes
- Projects
- Key results areas
- Critical success factors
- Performance indicators
- Measures of success
- Impact indicators
- Strategic plan
- Operational plan
- Development plan
- Business plan
- Financial plan

Some are always used in the same way by different authors and consultants, others are used differently by different

> **Box 2.1 Continued**
>
> people; some mean the same thing as each other, others overlap in their meaning. This makes it particularly hard for the unsuspecting voluntary organisation which has heard about strategic planning and assumes that there is some agreed terminology and way of doing it. Why is life never that simple? However, it is possible to get past the confusion over terminology and get down to the essentials of what strategic planning and management are all about.

So what is strategic planning and management?

There are many definitions of 'strategy', many of them very unhelpful from a voluntary sector point of view. One useful definition however comes from Craig and Grant (1993) who define strategy as 'the unifying theme that gives coherence and direction to the actions and decisions of an organisation.' They argue that 'strategy provides the stability of consistent direction and orientation, while permitting the flexibility to adapt to changing circumstances.' Bryson (1988) defines strategic planning as 'a disciplined effort to produce fundamental decisions and actions that shape and guide what an organisation is, what it does, and why it does it.'

The key elements of the model that we will build up here is shown in Figure 2.1.

Strategic issues

Essentially the word 'strategic' indicates a number of things:

1. It is the long-term that is being considered (typically 3–5 years) not the short-term.
2. It is about the fundamental 'ends', vision or purpose of the organisation not just about tactics.
3. It is about the whole organisation not just one aspect of it, although the same techniques can be applied to one part.

24 Strategic planning and management

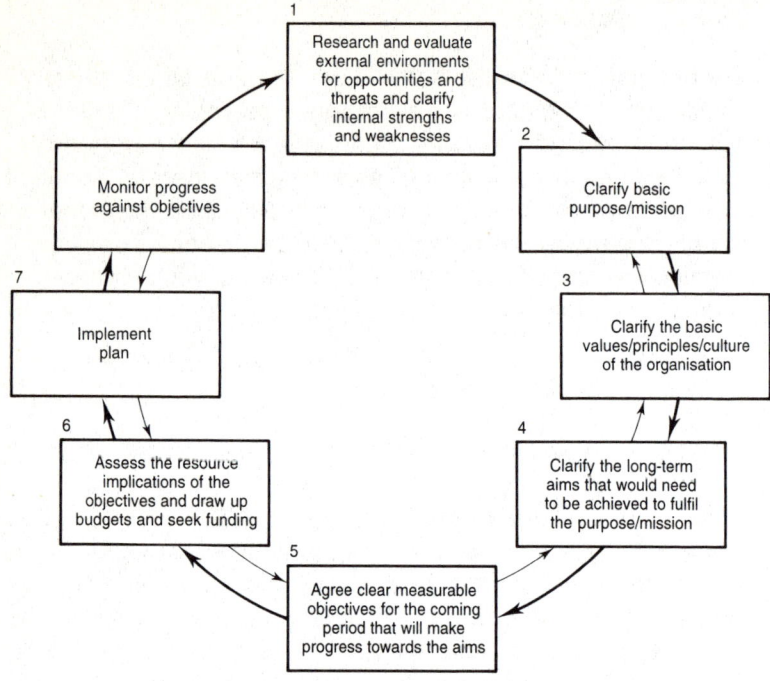

Figure 2.1 Strategic planning and management model.

4. It is about where an organisation sits in relation to its external environment (including other organisations) and how the external environment impacts on it. It is not only about internal factors.
5. It concerns the commitment of significant resources.
6. It is about making choices between different possibilities.

This chapter is specifically sub-titled 'Strategic planning and management' and the 'Management' part is important, although often neglected. The process is not only about how to draw up an appropriate plan for the future, but also about how to ensure that the plan achieves what it sets out to do, and how progress is monitored and adjusted against a continuously changing internal and external environment. Planning on its own is not enough. The management of the implementation, monitoring and review of the plans is also crucial.

Main strategic options

In essence an organisation providing services (or other activities) has a number of main strategic options:

1. Extend existing services to cover a new target group of potential beneficiaries.
2. Extend existing services to the current target group into new geographical areas.
3. Develop new services with the existing target group in the current geographical area.
4. Develop new services with a new target group in a new geographical area.
5. Extend existing services to the current target group in existing areas.
6. Develop new kinds of services in new areas.
7. Reduce or close existing services.
8. Improve existing services (see Chapter 4).

Doing nothing is rarely an option. Managing a voluntary organisation is rather like riding a bicycle. Once you stand still you tend to fall off. However, at a particular point in time the external threats may be so great that aiming for survival may indeed be the most appropriate option.

Essentially, a strategic planning and management process is the dynamic process of enabling an organisation to:

1. Create a broad long-term vision; and then
2. Move from a broad global vision to specific achievable and measurable objectives.
3. Move from a long-time frame to a shorter operational one.
4. Move from an overall vision for the organisation to specific objectives and programmes for specific parts (teams and individuals) of the organisation.

Where are we now?

Target group

The strategic planning process needs to begin with a formal or informal review or evaluation of where the organisation is now, before looking at the future. The first and most fundamental question in such a review can be asked in a number of different ways:

- Who does the organisation exist to serve?/help?
- Whose needs and aspirations does the organisation want to try and meet?
- Who are the target group of beneficiaries?
- What does the organisation want to change?

In answering these questions it is important to be as specific as possible. Clear definition of the primary target group of beneficiaries may include consideration of:

- Age group
- Gender
- Geographical boundaries
- Socio-economic group
- Abilities/disabilities
- Interests

Whether the organisation is in the field of service delivery, mutual support or campaigning it also needs to have clarity about the nature of the issue or problem that it is concerned with, e.g. mental health problems, unemployment, physical disability, lack of safe play areas, homelessness, sexual abuse, environmental destruction, etc. The greater clarity that it is possible to obtain the easier it is to try and meet the needs of specific beneficiaries.

An organisation concerned with 'mental health problems', for example, may be able to direct their work more effectively if they can be very specific about their target group of beneficiaries, e.g. 'the long-term supportive accommodation needs of young adults (17–25) from New Town who suffer from schizophrenia and have been referred by a social worker.'

Other stakeholders

The involvement of another agency (represented by the 'social worker' in the above example) also raises an important issue which needs to be considered. As well as the primary target group of beneficiaries, there are likely to be other agencies, particularly funders, policy makers, and Trustees, who have important expectations that need to be considered when trying to clarify the needs that the organisation is concerned with.

A 'stakeholder' can be defined as 'any person, group or organisation that can place a claim on an organisation's attention, resources, or output, or is affected by that output' (Bryson 1994).

A formal or informal review or evaluation, either at the beginning of the strategic planning process or after a period of implementation of a plan should concentrate on the needs and aspirations of both the beneficiaries and these other 'stakeholders' who have expectations of the work of the organisation, finding out what their problems or concerns are, what they think is done well or badly, and what they would hope to see in future. This process may be done by one-to-one structured interviews; by focus group discussions with key people; by written questionnaires; and/or by drawing on any research that has already been done.

The theme of involving the beneficiaries and other strategic planning stakeholders in the process of continuous improvement and in the decisions that may affect them is central to the main themes of this book and will be returned to continually.

Dreaming

Having started the process of clarifying the views and requirements of the beneficiaries and other stakeholders it is time for some dreaming; because planning is essentially dreaming with your eyes open. As Henry Mintzberg said in *The Rise and Fall of Strategic Planning*: 'many of the great strategies are simply great visions . . . only when we recognise our fantasies can we begin to appreciate the wonders of reality!' (Mintzberg 1994)

What is the long-term vision of and for the beneficiaries? Don't worry about whether it is going to be attainable in reality. It is trying to establish a very long-term goal that will provide focus and direction for the organisation over a long time period. What would the world (or at least the part that you're concerned with) look like if the organisation was successful?

Asking these fundamental questions on a regular basis and actively listening to the views of the beneficiaries and other stakeholders often makes an organisation realise that the previously stated view of the purpose of the organisation is no longer relevant, or is not clear, or that there are conflicting requirements from different stakeholders that need to be resolved. These realisations can be painful for an organisation and every organisation will contain individuals who particularly cherish the past and will try and resist change.

Asking the questions on pages 26 and 27 should provide most of the key information that an organisation needs to start to draw up a mission statement. This is basically a short (typically a few sentences) statement that will both inform those inside and outside the organisation as to what the organisation is and is trying to achieve, and also inspire them to work with energy and commitment towards achieving this vision.

A Mission statement should:

1. Be understandable, brief and concise;
2. Clarify the fundamental purpose of the organisation;
3. Create a clear vision of what the organisation wants to achieve in the very long-term;
4. Clarify the things that the organisation does well and that do the most good;
5. Encapsulate what is distinctive about the organisation;
6. Be motivating – creating passion and enthusiasm. It should encapsulate the reason people want to come to work;
7. Be consistent with the principles and values underlying the work of the organisation (see below);
8. Clarify the primary target group of beneficiaries and the commitment to meeting the needs;
9. Clarify the geographical scope;
10. Avoid excluding important areas of the organisation's work;
11. Honour the past but look to the future.

Some mission statements from the voluntary sector are given in Box 2.2.

Although no mission statement is perfect, each of the statements in Box 2.2 do, at least to some extent, reflect the various aspects of Peter Drucker's requirements for a good mission statement:

They're clear, they make sense, they lift people's vision and they let each person working in the organisation feel that he or she can make a difference. (Drucker 1990)

Box 2.2

Mission statements

To offer services of the highest possible standard to people with mental health needs; inform and educate the public about mental health, and press for high standards in the provision of mental health services.

(NI Association of Mental Health)

The Save the Children Fund works to achieve lasting benefits for children within the communities in which they live, by influencing policy and practice based on its experience and study in different parts of the world. In all its work, Save the Children endeavours to make a reality of children's rights.

(Save the Children Fund)

To promote the well-being of all older people and help make later life a fulfilling and enjoyable experience.

(Age Concern England)

To help young people who would not otherwise have the opportunity to develop their self-confidence, achieve economic independence, fulfil their ambitions and contribute to the community through the medium of self-employment.

(The Princes Youth Business Trust)

WWF's Mission is to achieve the conservation of nature and ecological processes by:

- preserving genetic, species and ecosystem diversity
- ensuring that the use of renewable natural resources is sustainable now and in the longer term for the benefit of all life on earth
- promoting actions to reduce to a minimum pollution and the wasteful exploitation and consumption of resources and energy

WWF's ultimate goal is to stop, and eventually reverse the accelerating degradation of our planet's natural environment, and to help build a future in which humans live in harmony with nature.

(World Wide Fund for nature)

Box 2.2 *continued*

The National Autistic Society aims to ensure that, by the year 2012 – the Society's 50th Anniversary – all those in the United Kingdom whose lives are affected by autism, or a related condition, receive services appropriate to their needs.
(National Autistic Society)

The NI Volunteer Development Agency promotes volunteering as a valuable and integral part of life in Northern Ireland. By providing a central resource of support, information and training to those who work with volunteers, the agency strives to improve the quality of volunteer involvement across all sectors.
(NI Volunteer Development Agency)

Help the Aged works to improve the quality of life of older people in the United Kingdom and internationally, particularly those who are frail, isolated or poor.
(Help the Aged)

Our mission is to enable individuals who have a disability to realise their potential, to exercise choice and control over their lives and to offer opportunities to those who wish to support them. In particular we support adults and young people who have learning disabilities or mental health problems.
(Mencap)

The importance of developing a mission statement that fulfils these criteria is illustrated by Nicholas Hinton, the former Director General of Save the Children Fund when he said:

Our mission statement, agreed upon a number of years ago, has probably done more to contribute to our planning, and especially our planning for growth, than any other single factor. (Hinton 1993)

Values

Alongside the organisation's vision of where it wants to get to in the long-run, (and sometimes incorporated into it), needs to be a view of the fundamental values, principles, philosophy or

---

Box 2.3

Values/principles

The following are some of the key words that frequently recur in statements of values/principles:

- High standards;
- Excellence;
- Effectiveness;
- Efficiency;
- Equity;
- Fairness;
- Appropriateness;
- Accountability;
- Accessibility;
- Openness;
- Redress;
- Easy to use complaints;
- Client/customer focus;
- Continuity;
- Normalisation;
- Equal opportunities;
- Partnership;
- Empowerment;
- People development;
- Team work;
- Choice;
- Privacy;
- Respect;
- Responsiveness;
- Clear information;
- Plain english.

These may not only concern how an organisation should be relating to its beneficiaries but also the trustees, staff and volunteers within the organisation and even other agencies.

culture of the organisation. The mission statement is essentially about 'ends' – where the organisation wants to get to. The statement of values or principles is more about the 'means', it is about the core philosophy that underpins the way things are done, or should be done in the organisation. With the Citizen's Charter Initiative and the hundreds of charters that have flowed from it, and publications such as *Home Life* concerned with the values that should be given priority in residential homes, the concept of a statement of values or principles has become fairly common.

Culture

These values are sometimes called the 'culture' of an organisation, or 'the way we do things round here'. More precisely, these statements form what is sometimes called the high-profile culture, i.e. the formal statements of the values that the organisation says it considers to be important. This of course is not to say that these are the values that are held to throughout the organisation. Careful probing, particularly by an outsider, often reveals a very different culture, the 'low-level' culture, which is what really happens.

The crucial task, having created a statement of values/principles (and this process should involve as many people in an organisation as possible) is to find ways to ensure that it underpins all aspects of the work, throughout the organisation, so that everyone instinctively lives the values, or to put it another way, that the high-level and low-level cultures are as similar as possible.

Policies

In bringing these principles or values to life it is likely that an organisation will need to develop a number of policies which explain the organisation's view of key principles/values and what their implications are for the work of the organisation.

Typically these major policies might include:
- Equal opportunities;
- Staff development (+ management development);

- Confidentiality;
- Staff conduct/Code of Practice;
- Quality;
- Complaints;
- Disciplinary;
- Grievance;
- Client rights;
- Employee communications;
- Health and safety;
- Communications.

The task of reviewing and clarifying the core values/principles can also in turn create a change to the mission statement. There may be particular values/principles which are so important or distinctive to the organisation that they should be incorporated into the mission statement.

In summary the values/principles of an organisation should:

1. Make clear *how* the organisation wants to work;
2. Clarify the relationship the organisation wishes to have with its beneficiaries;
3. Clarify the organisation's approach to its own trustees, staff and volunteers;
4. Be understandable, brief and concise;
5. Be consistent with the mission statement;

Figure 2.2 Strategic pyramid stage 1.

6. Include all the key values that are important throughout the organisation;
7. Create an impetus to continual improvement;
8. Acknowledge the diversity of individuals;
9. Help people feel involved, valued and proud to work for the organisation.

Having clarified a draft statement of the fundamental mission and values/principles of the organisation, the next step is to break the mission down into specific goals or aims.

However, before an organisation tries to draw up a number of specific long-term aims it needs to look at the factors that might influence what these aims should be. These factors might be internal or external, and might be positive or negative. Reviewing these factors is sometimes called a SWOT analysis (strengths, weaknesses, opportunities and threats).

Box 2.4

Principles/values

SENSE believes that everyone:

- Has rights and responsibilities and is entitled to dignity and respect.
- Has the right to quality services to meet individual needs.
- Has the right to opportunities which will promote individual development.
- Has the right to information.
- Has the right to make choices.
- Should be able to contribute to the development of services directly or through a representative, family member or advocate.

Barnardo's values:

- Respecting the unique worth of every person.
- Encouraging people to fulfil their potential.
- Working with hope.
- Exercising responsible stewardship.

Box 2.4 *continued*

Scope beliefs:
- We believe that every individual has a right to control his or her own life and to share in the opportunities, enjoyment, challenges and responsibilities of everyday life.
- We believe that care and concern for each and every person and respect for their human rights is central to any caring community.
- We believe that people with a disability are handicapped by the attitudes of others, at home, in the community, at work, and in national and local government.

United Response was founded upon christian principles and welcomes all individuals committed to working with people who have a disability and who support the following values statement:

1. We believe that all individuals, whatever their age, race, sex, religious belief or disability, should have the same rights and opportunities. We also recognise that each one of us requires help and advice with certain aspects of our lives.
2. United Response is therefore committed to:
   (a) Providing professional, creative and imaginative services delivered with dignity and respect that are based upon the needs and wishes of each user of our services.
   (b) Ensuring that individuals have as much control over their own lives as possible whilst recognising that some people have difficulty in making an informed decision.
   (c) Promoting positive images of people with disabilities thereby enhancing their self-esteem whilst improving attitudes in society generally.
   (d) Ensuring that individual rights, needs and wishes are met sensitively. We encourage the role of friends/ advocates and relatives in the decision making process.
   (e) A regular process of review of all our services.

> **Box 2.4** *continued*
>
> (f) Enabling individuals to enjoy a range of experiences and opportunities by participating in and contributing to their local community.
> (g) Providing a stimulating and supportive environment that respects the contribution of everyone that lives or works within the organisation.
> (h) A continued awareness of national care and legislative initiatives that is reflected in our contribution to the development of high quality services.

The analysis of external and internal factors outlined below may well have been carried out as part of a formal or informal review or evaluation at the beginning of this process, even before creating or reviewing the mission statement and statement of values/principles. As pointed out elsewhere, strategic planning is not a straight line process where one stage comes neatly after another, but a circular or feedback loop model where each part may have a significant influence on all the other parts.

External factors

If we start with external factors we need to consider at least the following:

1) Beneficiaries

The organisation needs to be aware of the trends in terms of the target group of actual or potential beneficiaries, as these are absolutely vital both in establishing the case for support from others and in drawing up plans for how their needs can be met most effectively. This might involve drawing on the latest research to clarify the number and nature of people within the target group: the trends in terms of numbers, gender, age, etc., and their needs and aspirations. This is absolutely crucial in determining not only the extent/size of provision needed, but also the appropriate standards of provision to fulfil these needs and aspirations which will change over time (see Chapter 4).

2) Social trends

In addition to the trends in relation to the target group of beneficiaries there may also be important social trends that affect the organisation and which need to be predicted for the future.

3) Government

It is vital to be aware of both the current and possible future legislative framework, as it relates to the target group or the key issue the organisation is concerned with, and also the current and possible future policies and practices of the relevant statutory agencies. These may represent both opportunities, for example, for new contracting arrangements, and threats, such as the withdrawal of grants, or new, potentially damaging, legislation.

4) Other organisations

Other organisations (voluntary, private and public sector) provide both opportunities for creating new partnerships, formal and informal, and also threats in that they may be planning to withdraw support or have plans which conflict with the organisation.

5) The economy

Changes in the economy may also have a crucial impact on the organisation's actual and potential beneficiaries, on its fund-raising and its ability to carry out its mission.

These are just some of a whole host of areas where there may be important changes taking place which may positively or negatively affect the possibility of achieving the goals of the organisation.

It is invaluable to spend some time thinking about all the external factors impinging on the organisation and analysing what changes are likely or possible and what may represent the most significant opportunities and threats. This analysis may have vital implications for the strategy that is eventually agreed.

Another useful technique, similar to a SWOT analysis, for analysing the external and internal factors impacting on the mission/vision of the organisation, or indeed any proposed change, is force field analysis (Figure 2.3). This model weighs the 'enabling' factors (internal and external) against the 'inhibiting' factors (internal and external) in order to be able to look at how to enhance the 'enablers' and tackle the 'inhibitors'. The size of the arrows in Figure 2.3 can be used to indicate the strength of the factor.

The key assumptions about the external environment should be made explicit in the organisation's plan, so that it is possible to assess the impact if the assumptions turn out to be wrong.

For each assumption it is necessary to ask the following questions:

1. What is the basis for this assumption? Why is it believed that it will happen?
2. What is the estimated probability, likelihood or risk of it happening or not happening?
3. What is the impact on the organisation if it does or doesn't happen?
4. What is the contingency plan if it does or doesn't happen?
5. At what point does a decision need to be made to implement the contingency plan?
6. How best can the reality be monitored against the assumptions?

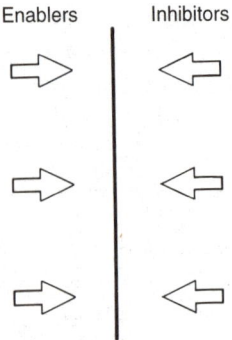

Figure 2.3 Force field analysis.

On the basis of these answers it is possible to develop a grid which relates the likelihood of an assumption taking place or not taking place to the impact on the organisation (Figure 2.4).

Issues impact analysis grid

Impact on organisation

		High	Medium	Low
Likelihood	High	Priority action	Action	Monitor effects
	Medium	Action	Contingency plan	Track
	Low	Contingency plan	Track	Track

Figure 2.4 Issues impact analysis grid (adapted from Peters 1993).

This then indicates when specific action needs to be taken, particularly when the likelihood of the assumption being wrong is high and the impact on the organisation of it being wrong is also high. In other situations all that may be required is to track the assumption, particularly where the potential impact of an incorrect assumption is relatively low.

It is also important to be aware of what can and what can't be controlled and the things somewhere in the middle, where an organisation may be able to have some influence (Figure 2.5).

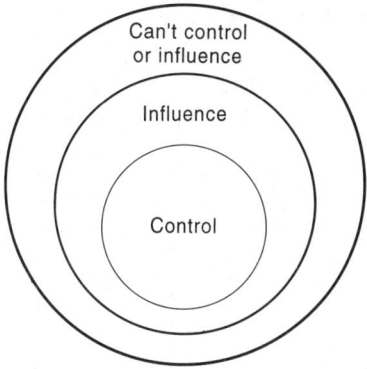

Figure 2.5 Three circles of control and/or influence (adapted from Peters 1993).

This latter area of advocacy or campaigning is an important one for many voluntary organisations.

Internal factors

However, as well as external factors to consider there are also important internal factors which will have a significant influence on future plans. These factors may be strengths to be built on or weaknesses which need to be ameliorated in some way.

These factors might include some of the following:

- Public image;
- Involvement of respected individuals;
- Expertise;
- Value for money;
- Quality of services;
- Promotion of equal opportunities;
- Volunteers;
- Staff;
- Relationship with funders;
- Relationship with decision-makers;
- Supporter base;
- Premises;
- Geographical coverage;
- Technology;
- Research capability;
- Systems and procedures;
- Commitment to training;
- The knowledge/commitment of the trustees.

The strengths and weaknesses of each organisation will be different. It can be tremendously valuable for trustees, staff and volunteers to spend some time trying to clarify the key strengths and weaknesses which may have important implications for the future, also asking the beneficiaries for their perspective on the relevance and effectiveness of the services provided. Other agencies who have an interest in or contact with the organisation should also be asked for their perspective on the strengths and weaknesses of the organisation.

The views of all these stakeholders can be crucial in developing a realistic picture. An organisation can often be taken in by its own PR and not see the real situation. Plans need to be built on an understanding of reality if they are to be successful.

The case study on pages 43 and 44 indicates the results of WWF's SWOT analysis of its marketing function.

We now have the first two parts of a model of strategic planning and management starting with a statement of mission and a statement of core values/principles, both of which may need to be amended in light of the analysis of internal strengths and weaknesses and external opportunities and threats above, and the specific expectations of the target group of beneficiaries and other key stakeholders.

Portfolio analysis

As part of the process of evaluating internal strengths and weaknesses it is important to analyse each of the existing programmes and projects of the organisation against some specific criteria. For example:

1. How much does the programme or project contribute towards achieving the mission and aims of the organisation: is it crucial? or only marginal? or does it make no contribution at all?
2. Is the need for the service increasing or decreasing?
3. How does the programme or project shape up in terms of the quality of service that is provided? Does it represent an example of best practice, or would it be perceived by others as being outdated or of poor quality?
4. Are there other organisations already meeting or capable and willing to meet the need?
5. Does the programme or project reflect the particular strengths of the organisation and its staff and volunteers?
6. Is the programme or project well funded or generate significant income from its activities, or is it a constant struggle to find the resources to keep it going?
7. Does the programme or project reflect an area of work that there is high or rising public and/or government concern, or is there little sympathy or support for this work?

Answers to these questions should start to indicate which of the existing programmes and projects should be expanded, developed, improved, contracted, or even terminated.

The Boston Consultancy group (see Bowman and Asch 1987) developed a simple matrix for this kind of portfolio analysis, which has been adapted in Figure 2.6 for a voluntary sector context.

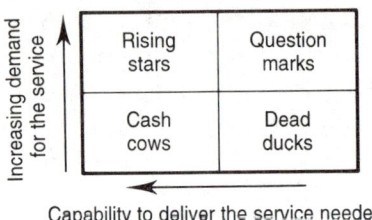

Rising stars: have real potential for growth and development with increasing popular and/or government support.

Question marks (or problem children): have the potential to make a significant contribution to the mission and aims, but are currently problematic.

Cash cows: reliable well-funded programmes or projects that provide a secure base for the organisation.

Dead ducks: use up valuable resources but make no real contribution to the organisation's mission.

Figure 2.6 Portfolio analysis matrix.

Services often tend to follow a standard life cycle (Figure 2.7).

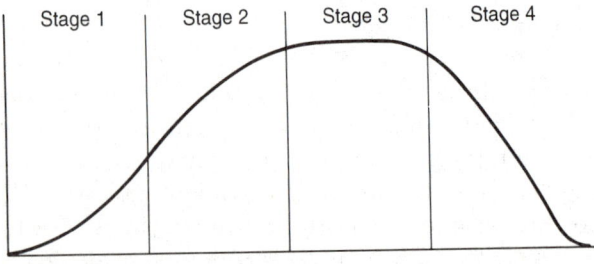

Figure 2.7 Service life cycle.

New services often begin as 'question marks' or 'problem children' and require a lot of attention to get off the ground. If early problems are sorted out and the rising demand is met by the capabilities of the organisation the service may become a rising star, although still requiring significant support. At the third stage the service capably meets the need and the main financial and other difficulties have already been sorted out so it requires little attention. However, all services eventually outlive their usefulness as the needs and aspirations of beneficiaries change. These 'dead duck' services need to be discarded to enable the organisation to concentrate on other 'question marks' and 'rising stars'.

The difficulty is knowing at which point in the cycle the service currently is, as any of the stages may be short or long. It is particularly problematic for an organisation which is dependent on one or two services which are at the stage 3 'cash cow' stage, but has not been able to develop any 'rising stars'.

Case study WWF UK SWOT analysis: key areas – marketing

Strengths	Weaknesses
Image	Image
Logo	Small membership
Charity	Poor lists
Emotive appeal	Communications
Visual appeal	Inadequate intermediaries
Achievements	Transience of fashion
Communications	Reference to costs: income ratio
Schools lecture service	
Flexible	Conservatism
Technical support	Inadequacy of follow through
Diverse	Lack of innovation
In fashion	Lack of physical resources
Cost: income ratio	Scientific inflexibility
Recognition of need	Inadequate market penetration
Awareness of market research	
Unique	No active conservation
Caravan	No audio-visual equipment
	Photographic resources

Case study *continued*

Opportunities	Threats
£700 given to charity in 1977	Competition
Schools	Legislation
Legislation	Economic climate
Better positioning	
Current events	
Economic climate	
Untapped sources	
Growing awareness of conservation importance	

Long range planning Vol 21 Feb 1988

But clear statements of mission and values/principles will not on their own mean that the organisation will necessarily get where it wants to go or in the way that it says it should. It is necessary to find steps to move from the Global and long-term towards the practical day-to-day work. As Peter Drucker has said:

A Vision is only a dream until it degenerates into work!

Long-term aims

The next step is to break the mission statement down into a number (usually between four and ten) of long-term aims/goals which, if they were achieved, would fulfil the mission. These aims should also reflect the agreed values/principles, and the critical assumptions about the future. They should also be bold and compelling. Indeed Collins and Parras (1994) in *Built to Last – successful habits of visionary companies* argue that the best way to stimulate progress is to set what they call 'BHAGS' (pronounced bee-hags), that is 'big, hairy, audacious goals'. Ambiguous aims won't inspire anyone to give of themselves.

Examples of long-term aims are contained in Box 2.5 on pages 45 and 46.

Box 2.5

Aims

The NI Volunteer Development Agency aims to:
- Promote volunteering in Northern Ireland.
- Promote good practice when involving volunteers.
- Promote the development of policy in relation to volunteering.
- Encourage debate on matters related to volunteering.
- Identify and analyse current trends in volunteering.
- Establish and maintain networks of organisations involving volunteers.

SENSE aims to:
- Provide a range of quality services across the UK including family support, children's services, residential and community services, continuing education, and advocacy.
- Work to develop new projects and services, either as an organisation or in partnership with others.
- Campaign for greater public, political and legal recognition of needs and action to meet needs.
- Manage our operations – including fund-raising and finances – in the most effective manner.

Mencap aims* to ensure that:
- The general public of all ages are aware of the potential, wishes and concerns of people with learning disabilities, and accept them as individuals with rights to be respected, obligations to meet and contributions to make to their local communities.
- Those making and implementing policies, or allocating resources with implications for people with learning disabilities are informed about, and responsive to, their needs.

> **Box 2.5** *continued*
>
> - Mencap local societies and Gateway Clubs and other affiliates are supported in their information, campaigning and service activities in their own localities, and their insights and concerns brought into the corresponding activities of Royal Mencap.
> - Mencap itself provides services in support of individuals and their families where such services can best be provided by the Royal Society, fit appropriately into the wider network of services and are adequately resourced to sustain high quality.
> - Those responsible for the standards of service, and for training and management of staff, give priority to the quality of the support and the choices and opportunities available to people with learning disabilities.
>
> * Mencap call these objectives.

To be most effective, such aims should:

1. Be understandable, brief and concise;
2. Cover all the main functions of the organisation, but not be overlapping;
3. Create challenging goals for the long-term future;
4. Be necessary and sufficient to fulfil the mission statement;
5. Be clearly about results/outcomes *not* activities;
6. Be consistent with the organisation's principles/values;
7. Avoid excluding important hoped for results/outcomes;
8. Only contain one idea in each aim.

As well as these very long-term 'visionary' aims, some strategic plans also contain a statement of priorities for the period of the strategic plan (e.g. three or five years). These priorities will be more specific and realistic than the long-term aims, but won't be as specific and timetabled as detailed objectives.

For example, the case study on p. 47 gives the key priorities for marketing in the WWF UK following their detailed SWOT analysis.

Case study WWF UK strategies, key area marketing

1. We will increase our membership and improve services to members.
2. We will increase the number and yield effectiveness of supporters' groups.
3. We will undertake a research programme to ascertain the best marketing opportunities in schools and will then increase fund-raising in this sector.
4. We will increase the yield effectiveness of commercial promotions and licensing.
5. We will liaise closely with WWF International to improve the yield effectiveness in the United Kingdom of international promotions.
6. We will make a concerted effort to increase substantially our income from business and charitable trusts.
7. We will improve the profitability of our trading operations and will search for new ways of increasing income from trading opportunities.
8. We will ensure that we are able to take advantage of special opportunities for raising funds.
9. We will build our lists in order to maximise fund-raising.
10. We will seek to further improve and widen our market image.
11. We will build up active key contacts in show business, commerce, and conservation and programme them centrally.
12. We will ensure that we have adequate and effective audio-visual equipment.
13. We will ensure that we use the caravan to the greatest advantage.
14. We will ensure that WWF photographic material is made more readily available for fund-raising purposes.
15. We will encourage donations in covenant form.
16. We will increase our share of the legacy market.

Our model might now look something like Figure 2.8.

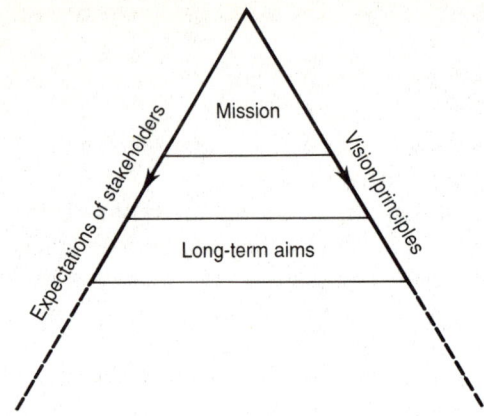

Figure 2.8 Strategic pyramid stage 2.

Measures of success

It is one thing having a broad statement of long-term aims and priorities, it is another to know how well they are being achieved. It is therefore vital to create some clear indicators or measures of success (sometimes called 'impact' or 'performance indicators') which help the organisation know how well it is doing in working towards each aim. These measures should be both valid (measure what they are intended to) and reliable (accurate and consistent).

Performance indicators can also be useful in reflecting how well the organisation is living up to its statement of agreed values/principles.

The more these indicators reflect the final outcome of the services provided for the beneficiaries the better, but the outcomes of services are often the most difficult to measure, and it is therefore likely that a range of other performance indicators will also be developed.

There are a number of different types of performance indicators:

1) Final outcomes

These are ideal indicators which show the extent to which the relevant aspects of the lives of the beneficiaries have been changed in relation to the service provided. They require a clear and quantifiable assessment of the position before and after the intervention of the organisation.

2) Take up of services

These are indicators which show to what extent particular services have been used over a period, e.g. the number of individuals given advice, provided with temporary accommodation, attended evening classes, etc.

3) Beneficiary reaction

This generally involve surveys of 'customer satisfaction'. Regular surveys can establish a baseline to assess current and then future performance.

4) Financial indicators

These may be unit costs which can be compared with previous years or other organisations. Funders particularly like this kind of indication. Financial indicators may also include the generation of income from fund-raising, trading, consultancy, training, contracts or grants, etc.

5) Standards

An indicator may be the achievement of specific agreed quality standards, or the percentage of times a particular quality standard was achieved (see the following chapter on quality assurance and management).

6) Objectives

Making the strategic plan an operational reality will involve the establishment of clear and assessable objectives which if achieved will create progress towards the aims. The achievement of each of these objectives is also a measure of success.

7) Negative

Indicators can also be negative, such as the number of errors or failures, or the number of times people had to be turned away.

Case study

Youth Train, a voluntary organisation involved in the training of young people might include the following as measures of success:

- The number of trainees obtaining employment within 3 months of leaving.
- The number of trainees obtaining a full NVQ (or NVQ units).
- Measurable increases in literacy or numeracy of trainees with special needs.
- The number of trainees through the training course.
- The percentage of clients who successfully complete placements.
- The percentage of trainees who rate the course as 'highly beneficial' after three months.
- The percentage of trainees who drop out during the course without employment.
- The average cost per trainee.

It is important that whatever measures of success are chosen, the information: is relatively easy, and not too expensive, to collect; is easy to understand; demonstrates changes over which the organisation has some control; and actually demonstrates progress towards a particular aim.

Once performance measures have been chosen that accurately reflect progress towards achieving the aims, it should be possible to start to create targets or standards to aim for using each measure. The ability to set accurate targets will improve with experience, but it is important not to start by setting them too low.

From his extensive experience Drucker argues that in managing the non-profit organisation 'as in other organisations it is crucial that performance standards are set high; you cannot ease into them gradually. If you start low, you'll probably not be able to go higher because your people will view the original standards as the norm' (Drucker 1990).

There is also a danger of setting them unrealistically high so that those responsible for achieving them feel constantly demotivated by aiming for targets they know they can never attain.

Objectives

Having now established some long-term aims and some measures to assess how successfully the organisation is working towards achieving these aims, we now need to look at each of these aims and establish some clear assessable objectives or accomplishments which can be achieved within a specific time frame.

In an ideal and very stable world it may be possible to establish objectives to be achieved in each of the three or five years of a strategic plan. Each year a report could be produced which shows the achievement or otherwise of these objectives. Certainly, the more specific and realistic the objectives which can be established for future years the better. However, the reality for most organisations is that the environment in which they are working is changing so rapidly and the availability of funding is so insecure that it is often very difficult to be too specific about plans much more than perhaps a year or two away.

With organisations often required to submit funding applications, or negotiate for contracts, perhaps up to six months prior to the start of their financial year, it is necessary to have by then very clear objectives for the following financial year and to have the resource implications of these objectives assessed and costed. Work on these objectives is likely to be annual and started perhaps around six months before the financial year to which they relate.

So what are the characteristics of a good objective? Objectives should be SMART:

- Specific and stretching;
- Measurable, or at least it should be possible to assess to what extent it has been achieved;
- Achievable – it is important to be realistic. Objectives also need to be allocated to a specific team or individual, and agreed by those who have to carry them out;
- Relevant to the appropriate aim and also realistic in terms of the available resources and the ability to achieve it;
- Time-scaled so it is clear by when it is to be achieved, and timely in the sense that the time-scale established is sensible.

> **Case study Objectives for an advice and training centre**
>
> For Orangetree advice and training centre to say that it is going 'to increase the level of skill in advice-giving' would be a rather poor objective as it is too general and difficult to assess progress against.
>
> To be more specific and to say that it intends 'to run three courses on advice-giving by 31 March 1996' would be better.
>
> 'To provide advice-giving training to 50 individuals by 31 March 1996' would be even better.
>
> 'To enable 50 individuals to achieve NVQ level 2 in Advice, guidance, counselling and psychotherapy by 31 March 1996' would be still better.
>
> To enable 50 individuals to achieve NVQ level 2 in Advice guidance, counselling and psychotherapy by 31 March 1996 at a cost per person not exceeding £500, is starting to approach the ideal.

Because of resource constraints it may not be possible for an organisation to achieve all of its objectives. It is important to identify those objectives that the organisation should put most time and energy into. On the pareto principle that 20% of the effort will produce 80% of the results, it is therefore this 20% of effort that needs to be given priority attention.

One method of prioritising is to allocate the objectives to one of three groups, as follows:

1. High priority: Must-do's – survival objectives.
2. Medium priority: Ought-to-do's – key improvement objectives.
3. Low priority: Nice-to-do's – optional improvement objectives.

The model should now look something like Figure 2.9.

Figure 2.9 Strategic pyramid stage 3.

Plans and programmes

These operational objectives need to be made real by the drawing up of detailed action plans which specify how the objectives will be achieved. These plans or programmes should also have within them their own intermediate targets, i.e. milestones on the way to achieving the specific objectives. Many of these intermediate targets are likely to be delegated to specific individuals or teams.

In drawing up specific programmes there are a number of key points:

1. Are the programmes clearly linked to the objectives? Will they bring about the desired result by the agreed timescale?
2. Have all the different ways of achieving the objective been considered? Is there perhaps a better method than the one currently used?
3. Have examples of 'best practice' elsewhere been looked at? What other organisations achieve the same objectives most effectively and efficiently (a process sometimes known as 'benchmarking')?
4. Have contingency plans been drawn up of what to do if key assumptions turn out to be wrong?
5. What resource, funding and fund-raising implications do different types of programmes have?

The model should now look something like Figure 2.10:

Figure 2.10 Strategic pyramid stage 4.

Resources

As well as looking at what the organisation wants to achieve and the plans and programmes needed to achieve its objectives, it is also necessary to consider the resources that will be needed to carry out the plans. These resources fall into three main groups:

- People;
- Material/physical resources;
- Finance.

In fact it is only the first two that are involved in carrying out the plans, but it is the third that pays for the other two (Figure 2.11).

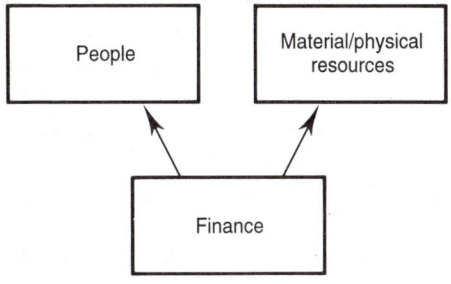

Figure 2.11 Resources.

Human resources

For most voluntary organisations by far the most important resource is the people. They are the key to achieving the organisation's aims and meeting the needs of its beneficiaries. It is crucial therefore to regularly (at least annually) review the human resource needs of the organisation on the basis of the strategic aims and objectives of the organisation. These human resources may include a combination of any of the following:

- Full-time;
- Part-time;
- Permanent;
- Temporary;
- Employed;
- Self-employed;
- Consultants;
- Front-line;
- Support;

- Managers;
- Volunteers;
- Trainees;
- Placements;
- Trustees.

As well as considering the number and type of roles required to carry out the plans of the organisation the human resource strategy needs to assess the appropriate structure within which the people should work to best achieve the results desired. It is also necessary to ensure that there are the leadership and the management systems to motivate the staff and volunteers, and to carry the plans through. It is crucial too to assess the skills and knowledge required by the people in those roles in order to achieve the aims and objectives and plan how these training needs will be met. This issue is dealt with in greater length in Chapters 5 and 6.

The review of human resource needs is sometimes carried out under the '5 Ss'

- Staff (including volunteers);
- Structures;
- Systems (e.g. how pay is determined, communication and decision-ımaking systems, etc.);
- Style (this relates to the values/principles of the organisation and the kind of culture that the organisation wants;
- Skills (Training needs).

The costs involved in employing people are likely to include recruitment costs, salary costs, National Insurance contributions (NIC), pension contributions, travel costs, induction and training, expenses, plus the costs involved in just carrying out their job. Volunteers will incur some of these costs too, although not salary, NIC, or pension costs. Consultants will charge fees (which may include VAT) and other expenses, which should be agreed from the outset.

Material/physical resources

In addition to the people, the organisation will need to make use of a range of material/physical resources to achieve its plans. These resources will be different for every organisation but might include the following:

- Buildings;
- Equipment;
- Computers (hardware and software);
- Vehicles;
- Furniture;
- Fittings;
- Curtains and carpets;
- Publications;
- Stationery;
- Fuel (heat, light, power);
- Food;
- Telephone;
- Post and printing.

The material/physical resources needed will include a mixture of one-off capital items which will last for a number of years, and revenue items which will involve expenditure every year and which are used within that year (consumables). A capital item may become a revenue item if it is leased or rented, instead of being bought outright, and capital expenditure on, say equipment, may also have significant revenue implications, e.g. operating costs, maintenance contracts, which need to be properly thought through.

Finance

Once both the human and material resources needs have been reviewed it is possible to start to put together a budget which puts a price tag on these plans. This budget should include both income and expenditure estimates, if possible, for each of the following two to three years. It should provide:

1. A basis for discussion with statutory funders/purchasers.
2. Targets for income to be generated from other sources (i.e. projected expenditure less assured income).
3. A basis on which to re-assess objectives and plans in light of the cost implications.

4. A basis in which to look at ways of achieving the organisation's objectives and quality standards, but at a lower cost.
5. A basis for a contingency plan if the necessary income cannot be generated.
6. A basis for drawing up a monthly cash flow projection, so that a serious financial shortfall, perhaps caused by the timing of when grants are received, or seasonal factors in fund-raising income, can be predicted and either avoided altogether or the impact softened.
7. A basis to continually monitor progress (income and expenditure) throughout the year, with the production of regular management accounts often quarterly or monthly which compare budgeted projections with what happened in practice. This enables problems of overspend or income shortfalls to be detected early and appropriate action taken.

For more detailed information in this area *Financial Management for Charities and Voluntary Organisations* by Keith Manley (1994) ICSA is strongly recommended.

Monitoring

There not only needs to be a clear plan for the future, but also, some way of monitoring the progress against the agreed aims and objectives (not only finance) and taking corrective action as necessary. Indeed experiences at one level of the planning model may have important implications for one or more of the other levels, e.g. difficulties in implementing one of the detailed plans may result in a change to the deadline for achieving the relevant objective.

Having established what the measurable indicators of success will be (see above), including the operational objectives, what is now required is to put in place the key elements of monitoring and review, which should happen at three different levels:

1. There needs to be a system of progress reporting to ensure that the plans and programmes are being carried out in line with the agreed targets and that the objectives will therefore be achieved by the agreed deadlines. These progress reports,

which might be produced, say, quarterly, should also indicate any corrective action necessary to get things back on course and also to give advance warning if a particular objective will not be achieved as agreed.
2. There also needs to be a process, probably annually or every six months, for evaluating the overall achievement of the operational objectives and analysing the measures of success. This review should then form part of the process of drawing up and agreeing the operational objectives for the coming year.
3. Every three to five years there also needs to be a process established to carry out a major evaluation of the overall progress towards achieving the mission and long-term aims, along with a major re-assessment of the external factors which may have a positive or negative impact on the organisation, and the organisation's internal strengths and weaknesses. This evaluation should then inform a review of the mission and long-term aims, which can then be revised for the new strategic planning period.

The model should therefore be complete as we start again at the top of the pyramid (Figure 2.12). However there is also a crucial

Figure 2.12 Strategic pyramid stage 5.

human side to creating and achieving plans that needs to be taken into account.

Commitment

Creating a detailed strategic planning and management framework is of limited value if the commitment within the organisation to carry it through has not been nurtured.

In all organisations, for all kinds of reasons, there will be some people who will resist change, not necessarily actively or obviously. Often the most damaging resistance is quiet and hidden. There are likely to be excuses why targets cannot be met due to 'lack of resources', 'overwork', 'lack of time', 'staffing problems', etc. or that the original plan was 'unrealistic' or 'over-ambitious'.

How can such problems be overcome or indeed avoided in the first place? Prevention is always better than cure and the key to commitment is giving the people who will be involved in carrying out the plan a real and active involvement in creating the plan, right from the beginning. Involve as many people as possible in creating the mission statement, in drawing up the statement of values/principles, in drafting the long-term aims and measures of success, the objectives and in subsequent reviews of plans. Show the trustees, staff and volunteers that their views are valued and they are not just carrying out the ideas of a few at the top. Including as many people as possible in this process creates a real sense of ownership. It is not just the plan that 'they' drew up, but *our plan*, the one 'we worked hard at together'. If they have been included, the trustees, staff and volunteers creating it will want to work hard at achieving the plan and removing hurdles that get in the way, rather than creating them. This enthusiasm and energy is likely to be very contagious and encourage others who might be not quite so positive.

Box 2.6

Everett Rogers, an American Academic, has suggested a number of other factors that are important in helping people accept change:

Box 2.6 *continued*

Perceived advantage

How much better is the change than what happened before, and is it worth the extra effort? Your aim should be to demonstrate the advantage of implementing plans to those who implement them. If you can, they are more likely to follow the intended strategy rather than some different one.

Compatibility

How compatible is what is being suggested with what happens now? If it involves little change and disruption it is far more likely to be accepted than if it involves a high degree of change.

Communicability

How easy is it to communicate what you want to happen in a way that people can understand and relate to? If it isn't, you will have a hard job putting it across to an audience.

Adapted from Peters (1993).

Box 2.7

There is no right way to start a strategic planning process. How long you will need and who should be involved will depend on the size of your organisation; how much previous strategic planning work has been undertaken and when; how much consensus there is within the organisation about the goals of the organisation; and how much time trustees, staff and volunteers can give to the process. Here however is an

Box 2.7 *continued*

example of the planning programme of one organisation over a six month period.

1. Steering group established, representing different parts of the organisation.
2. Plan for the strategic planning process agreed.
3. One day meeting of trustees, staff volunteers and beneficiaries to discuss the plan, assess the needs and aspirations of the beneficiaries, draw up draft mission statement values, and long-term aims.
4. Steering group meeting to refine mission, values and aims (for further consultation with the full group and then the executive committee).
5. One day meeting of full group (partly in mixed sub-groups) to carry out a SWOT analysis.
6. Steering group meeting to refine key assumptions about the future and the implications, opportunities, threats and internal strengths and weaknesses (for further consultation with the full group).
7. One day meeting of full group (partly in functional sub-groups) to draw up 'Measures of Success' under each aim.
8. Steering group meeting to refine measures of success (for further consultation with full group).
9. One day meeting of full group (partly in functional sub-groups) to draw up specific objectives for the following financial year.
10. Steering group to refine draft objectives (for further consultation with full group).
11. One day meeting (partly in functional sub-groups) to consider all the resource implications of the agreed aims and objectives.
12. Steering group meeting to refine resource implications (for further consultation with full group).
13. Steering group meeting to create a draft monitoring system for consultation with full group.
14. Final meeting of full group to review and agree all previous work and monitoring system

Key points

The model of strategic planning and management presented in this chapter provides voluntary organisations with an adaptable framework to give 'coherence and direction to the actions and decisions of the organisation' through the following tasks:

- The analysis of the external environment and the opportunities and threats that it represents.
- The analysis of the particular strengths and weaknesses of the organisation.
- The development of a clear and coherent mission statement and long-term aims.
- The clarification of the distinctive values/principles that are important to the organisation in how it works.
- The establishment of assessable objectives and standards against which success can be measured.
- The analysis of the human, material and financial resources required to fulfil the organisation's aims and objectives.
- The development of a framework to monitor progress.

3 Performance management

Chapter summary

It is crucial that the work of individuals within an organisation is linked into the kind of aims and objectives highlighted in the previous chapter. Here, a performance management model is presented, which enables specific targets to be set with individual staff and volunteers in the light of the organisation's aims and objectives, and to be regularly reviewed. The model also enables individual's training and development needs to be assessed to ensure that they have the necessary skills to do the job.

Making plans effective

As indicated in the last section on 'Commitment', plans on their own are of no value. They only become useful if they are carried out by people. Often what happens is that the actual work that individuals do bears little relationship to any strategic or operational plans that exist. Indeed, staff and volunteers are often unclear about what results or outcomes are expected of them, despite the existence of organisational plans. If it is unclear what results or outcomes are expected then it is very difficult for the person themselves or anyone else to say whether they are doing a good job or not.

What is performance management?

Clarifying the relationship between the aims and priorities of the organisation as articulated in the planning process discussed above and the actual work of each individual involved in the organisation is sometimes called performance management. Unfortunately this expression is sometimes also used to refer to specific performance-related pay systems. It is interesting to note that over the last decade the introduction of performance-related pay systems has been a major trend in the private sector and increasingly in the public sector. However a series of recent research studies (for example, Marsden and Richardson 1991) have shown that there is very little evidence to support the contention that they improve work performance, except in a small proportion of tightly defined sales-orientated jobs. There is indeed plenty of evidence to the contrary. Richard Steenberg, writing in *Non-profit management and leadership* (1990) has effectively argued that performance-related pay schemes have 'unique disadvantages within the non-profit sector due to a lack of appropriate output measures and the potentially negative perspective of donors.' I also think that it is inappropriate for the voluntary sector because the primary motivation of the staff and volunteers is usually the cause they are working for, not money; performance related pay on the other hand assumes that money is the key motivator.

Performance management in the sense that it is used here has been defined as 'a process or set of processes for establishing shared understanding about what is to be achieved (and how it is to be achieved), and of managing people in a way that increases the probability that it will be achieved' (Frank Hartte 1994).

Performance management is not a 'top-down' process, but a shared and continuous process committed to improving the results of the work of teams and individuals and working relationships.

The basis of performance management is the simple proposition that 'when people know and understand what is expected of them, and have been able to take part in forming those expectations, they can and will perform to meet them (Armstrong 1994 *Performance Management*), a point that has already been stressed in relation to the organisational strategic planning process above.

Aims of performance management

Armstrong (1994) specifies the aims of performance management as to:

- achieve sustainable improvements in organisational performance;
- act as a lever for change in developing a more performance orientated culture;
- increase the motivation and commitment of employees;
- enable individuals to develop their abilities, increase their job satisfaction and achieve their full potential to their own benefit and that of the organisation as a whole;
- develop constructive and open relationships between individuals and their managers in a process of continuing dialogue which is linked to the work actually being done throughout the year;
- provide a framework for the agreement of objectives as expressed in targets and standards of performance so that mutual understanding of these objectives and the role both managers and individuals have to play in achieving them is increased;
- focus attention on the attributes and competencies required to perform effectively and on what should be done to develop them;
- provide for the accurate and objective measurement and assessment of performance in relation to agreed targets and standards so that individuals receive feedback from managers on how well they are doing;
- on the basis of this assessment, to enable individuals with their managers to agree improvement plans and methods of implementing them and jointly to review training and development needs and agree how they should be satisfied;
- provide an opportunity for individuals to express their aspirations and concerns about their work;
- provide a basis for rewarding people in relation to their contribution by financial and/or non-financial means; the former consisting of performance-related pay and the latter including recognition of achievement and opportunities to take on more responsibility or enhance knowledge and skills;

- demonstrate to everyone that the organisation values them as individuals;
- assist in empowering people – giving people more scope to take responsibility for and exercise control over their work;
- help to retain high quality people;
- support total quality management initiatives.

The performance management cycle should look something like Figure 3.1.

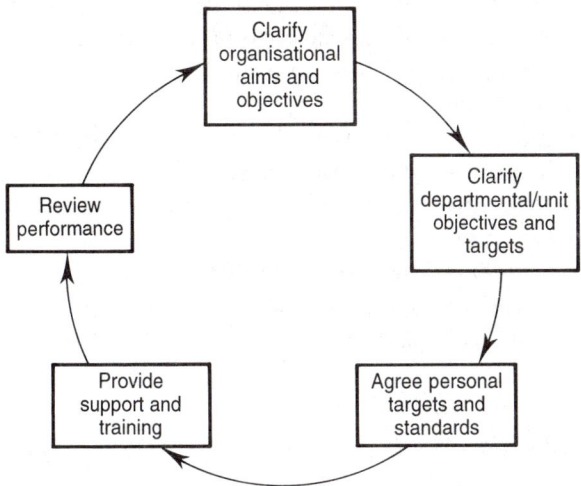

Figure 3.1 Performance management cycle.

Advantages for the individual

This process has many advantages for the individual:

1. It ensures that they can see their role within the 'big picture' and can see how their contribution fits into the whole.
2. They are fully involved in establishing appropriate targets.
3. They can receive whatever support and training (often on-the-job coaching) they need to carry out the role effectively.
4. They know how their performance will be measured, i.e. what success looks like and therefore how they are getting on.

5. They can be given challenges which stretch them but are attainable.
6. They can be given appropriate recognition.

Advantages for the organisation

The organisation also benefits, from:
1. All of the individuals contributing in a planned and focused way towards the aims and objectives of the organisation. The organisation's plans are cascaded down the organisation.
2. Having well-motivated staff who know both what they are doing and why.
3. Having staff and volunteers with the skills and knowledge to carry out their jobs effectively.
4. Its performance being monitored and corrective action being taken when necessary.
5. Its performance continuously improving.
6. The creation of an achievement-orientated culture.
7. Improved quality standards and improved consistency.

Implementation

So where does an organisation start in implementing a performance management process?

The first two stages of establishing clear organisational and departmental aims and objectives are vital and have already been dealt with in detail in Chapter 2.

Performance reviews

The next key point of the process is a regular planned meeting between the manager and the individual who is accountable to him/her. Such regular reviews can also be carried out as a team. Depending on the nature of the organisation, the job, the individual and how long they have been in post, review meetings are likely to be quarterly, bi-annually, or annually.

Common problems

In some organisations this meeting is known as the performance review or appraisal, but in practice is often an unsatisfactory and unedifying process for all involved. Some of the key problems in many schemes include the following:

1. It is often viewed as a one-way process from the manager to the individual. In one organisation known to the author it is known by the staff as the 'annual insult'!
2. Neither the manager nor the individual does any preparation.
3. It is linked to salary, so the concern is primarily with the financial implications.
4. Criticism is vague and personalised and therefore only perceived as negative.
5. Criticism has been held over and stored up for the appraisal/review which is therefore full of nasty surprises.
6. No clear targets or standards are set for the future.
7. The individual is not involved in developing the targets or standards – they are imposed from 'on high'!
8. The manager is unwilling or unable to be honest about performance that is below standard.
9. No arrangements are made for monitoring progress.
10. Training and development needs are not agreed or if they are, they do not take account of the priorities of the organisation or agreed competencies for the job (see Chapters 5 and 6).
11. The manager doesn't have the skills to coach individuals to enable them to develop their skills and knowledge.

Good practice

All these negative points about poor performance review/appraisal schemes give a good indication of the elements that need to be included in a good scheme. These include the following:

1. Ensure the managers know how to prepare for and carry out an effective performance review/appraisal process by effective training and have been appraised themselves.

2. Ensure the individuals to be reviewed/appraised know what to expect and how to prepare properly.
3. Ensure that sufficient notice has been given to allow time for proper preparation.
4. Ensure that sufficient time has been allowed in an uninterrupted, comfortable and private place.
5. Ensure that some time is spent reviewing together the job description and competency profile (see Chapters 5 and 6) of the post, in light of organisational and departmental aims and objectives.
6. The achievement of previously agreed targets is mutually identified (starting with the individual's view) and praised by the manager.
7. Targets not met and other problems will have been previously identified and discussed so there are no surprises. This performance review is an opportunity for a wider discussion to look at lessons learnt and how systems need to be improved to ensure future performance is satisfactory.
8. The development of clear and specific standards/competencies (see Chapters 5 and 6) enables the individual and the manager to identify specific strengths and weaknesses – strengths that can be built on and weaknesses that can be remedied by some form of training/development activity (often coaching). These ideas are explored more fully in Chapters 5 and 6.
9. It is crucial to the whole performance management process that clear targets and performance standards are set for the coming period that are consistent with and contribute to the aims and objectives of the organisation and are SMART (see p. 52).
10. Finally, it is important to establish when and how progress will be monitored, perhaps at monthly or fortnightly supervision sessions. The performance review/appraisal meetings should be seen as a part of the continual review of progress against the agreed targets and standards and not as an isolated event.

Figure 3.2 gives an example of a performance review/appraisal framework which is completed by both the manager and the individual before the performance review/appraisal meeting and is discussed during the meeting with the aim of reaching understanding and hopefully agreement, particularly on the ways forward.

Part 1

1. General details:

    Name: _____
    Job title: _____
    Manager: _____
    Project/unit: _____
    Date appointed: _____
    Date of last appraisal: _____

2. Job description: _____
    What changes need to be made to improve its relevance or clarity?
    _____

3. Achievements:
    What areas of the job have been performed well against the agreed standards and targets during the period?
    _____

4. Areas of concern:
    What standards or targets were not met? What lessons can be learnt for the future? Are there other areas of concern?
    _____

5. Overall assessment:
    Overall, how would you describe the work performance during the period?
    _____

6. Strengths:
    Main strengths – how can these be built upon?
    _____

7. Weaknesses:
    Main weaknesses – how can these be improved?
    _____

Figure 3.2 Performance review/appraisal framework.

Performance management

8. Training/development:
   What were the training/development activities undertaken in the last 6 months? What was learnt from them? What impact did they have on performance?
   _____

9. Training/development needs:
   What skills or knowledge need to be developed to help performance in the job? How might these be developed?
   _____

10. Career/ambitions:
    Longer term career ambitions – how can the organisation facilitate these?
    _____

11. Standards:
    What changes need to be made to the standards of performance expected to ensure they remain relevant, challenging, achievable and measurable for the coming period?
    _____

Part 2, Action plan

12. Targets:
    What are the specific targets over the coming period?

Target	Person responsible	Timing	Review date

Figure 3.2 continued.

Key points

Organisational plans are carried out by people as individuals and in teams. Performance management provides a framework for individuals to be involved in:

- Setting targets for their own work that will contribute to the organisation's aims and objectives.
- Monitoring progress towards achieving these targets.
- Identifying blockages that reduce the effectiveness of individuals, teams and the organisation.

4 Quality assurance and management

> Quality – you know what it is, yet you don't know what it is. But that's self-contradictory. But some things *are* better than others, that is, they have more quality. But when you try and say what quality is . . . it all goes poof! What the hell is quality? What is it?
>
> (Pirsig, 1974)

Chapter summary

In order to meet the needs of their beneficiaries on a consistent basis voluntary organisations need to develop both a culture of continuous improvement and systems for creating and monitoring specific quality standards. Quality is defined here as 'meeting agreed needs'. It is particularly the beneficiary, who is the recipient of the service, who should define what quality means for them.

This chapter suggests a process for drawing up quality standards to meet the needs and expectations of beneficiaries and for establishing procedures which ensures that these standards are met consistently. It explains the potential value and problems for voluntary organisations of BS EN ISO 9000 quality assurance system. Ways of ensuring that the culture of continuous improvement, often called total quality management, can be developed in voluntary organisations are given and one self-assessment framework for assessing progress in creating the quality culture is highlighted.

Quality of service

The previous chapter looked at how to make the organisation's vision of the future a reality. It was essentially about *what* the organisation should be doing in light of this vision and how to get there. The beneficiaries of the organisation and other stakeholders are, however, not only concerned with what the organisation does, but with *how* it does it.

Individuals seeking advice, for example, don't just want any old advice, they want accurate and relevant advice. They are also concerned about other aspects of the service that is provided: whether the staff are friendly and courteous; whether the surroundings are pleasant; whether they are kept waiting long, etc. These are all issues to do with the quality of the service provided.

Definition

From the outset, the word 'quality' can cause something of a problem: it can mean essentially two different things. It can be used to mean that something is of a high standard or grade as in 'the booklet that The Brookstone Tenants Association produced on tenants' rights was a quality production'. Used in this way it usually indicates that something is at the expensive, in this case glossy, end of the market, in the same way that a 'quality car' might be seen as a Rolls-Royce, Jaguar, BMW, etc. In the quality movement that has swept the World's private sector companies, however, the use of the word 'quality' maintains the concept of standards but removes the implication about what 'grade' or end of the market it represents. The only issue is whether it meets the needs of the person who will be using the service or product. So a duplicated A4 leaflet on tenants' rights might equally be a 'quality product' if it meets the needs of those who will be reading it. Indeed if the 'glossy' version is not in plain English or the language of the user, or is inaccurate, or is not relevant to the needs of tenants, it may indeed be only the duplicated A4 version that represents quality to the person reading it.

Common definitions of this meaning of quality include:

- Fitness for purpose or use (Juran and Gryna 1993);
- Conformance to requirements (Crosby 1984);
- Meeting the customer requirements (Oakland 1989);

- Meeting or exceeding customers' expectations at a price that represents value to them (Harrington, 1986).

The British Standards Institute provides a more comprehensive definition of quality as

The totality of features and characteristics of a product or service that bear on its ability to satisfy stated or implied needs (British Standard).

For the voluntary sector however a more concise and relevant definition might simply be 'satisfying agreed needs'.

Fundamentally what most voluntary organisations are about is meeting need, or enabling people to meet their own needs. Therefore the quality movement should be even more important to the voluntary sector than it has become for the private sector, which is primarily about making money and not first and foremost about meeting need.

Box 4.1

In helping your organisation start on the quality road it can be helpful to get all the key individuals together (which may include staff, volunteers, management committee members, and clients) and before giving them some of the standard definitions above ask them to individually come up with their own definition of 'quality'; put them together, perhaps on a flip chart; then try and pull out what are the key elements of all the suggested definitions.

The definition of 'satisfying agreed needs' leaves a number of questions unanswered. The first and most fundamental of these is; *whose* needs are the organisation trying to satisfy?

Voluntary organisations are set up for all kinds of reasons and to provide services (including campaigning or other activities) for many different types of beneficiaries: children; young people; old people; sick people; people who are dying; the disabled; the homeless; people with mental health or alcohol problems; the unemployed; animals – the list is endless and is constantly developing as new needs are identified. As stressed earlier when strategic planning was discussed, it is vital for all voluntary organisations to be clear about who the object of their services or other activities is, or will be, and where the boundaries to that group are. No one organisation can do everything, so it is vital if we are to respond well to the needs of our agreed target group that we are also clear about who we cannot help.

Many organisations face serious difficulties because they have not clearly determined the target group, or there is fundamental disagreement about this issue. When groups are in this position and try to be all things to all people they usually have difficulty agreeing priorities or standards and really satisfying any of the wide range of needs that they are trying to respond to. The quality of the services provided may well be perceived as low by many of the beneficiaries.

Box 4.2

It is a valuable exercise for organisations to list all the categories of people that the organisation wishes to respond to or reflect their needs and expectations. (These 'stakeholders' may include beneficiaries, funders, referral agencies, trustees, staff, volunteers, etc.) Try and be as specific as possible, so it is also clear who the organisation is not going to be in a position to help.

Once you have listed them, rank them in order of importance.

Having done this take the category of stakeholders that you have given top priority and list all the main needs and aspirations that they expect or hope you will be able to satisfy. Having done that, prioritise the list. Now do the same exercise for second highest stakeholders group and so on.

The second question that arises from the definition of quality as being 'to satisfy agreed needs' is: who should define what those needs are? The answer (and this is one of the clearest messages of the quality movement) is that the primary definers of those needs must be the people who are affected by those services or activities, i.e. the organisation's beneficiaries. As the leading authors on quality in the service sector conclude:

> The only criteria that count in evaluating service quality are defined by customers. Only customers judge quality; all other judgements are essentially irrelevant. Specifically service quality perceptions stem from how well a provider performs vis-à-vis customers' expectations about how the provider should perform. (Zeithaml *et al.* 1990, p. 16)

But of course no matter how perceptive and caring organisation's trustees, staff or volunteers may be, their list may not be the same as that of the organisation's beneficiaries. It is therefore vital that the views and aspirations of the beneficiaries are sought and clarified.

Box 4.3

It is possible to help the process of clarifying the views of the organisation's beneficiaries and other stakeholders by the following method.

For each of the main stakeholders above, list the ways that are currently used to assess their needs and expectations and suggest some additional, specific and practical ways that their views could be sought and clarified. Use these ideas to develop an active listening strategy so that it is ensured that the views and aspirations of the target group of beneficiaries (who often see themselves as powerless in society) and other stakeholders have been properly heard and taken account of.

It is the carrying out of an active listening strategy, whether through meetings, focus groups, questionnaires, structured interviews, or whatever, that is the fundamental basis of a quality initiative, because the beneficiaries are the individuals or groups who must define what their needs are, and therefore what quality should be for the organisation.

The word 'agreed' in our quality definition is also important, because there are likely to be needs and aspirations expressed by the target group which the organisation is either unwilling (perhaps for moral or legal reasons) or unable (perhaps due to resource or external constraints) to satisfy. It is therefore important to be very clear not only about who the target group is, but also about what the needs and expectations are that the organisation is planning to meet.

For example, the target group might be homeless young people in Newcastle, and it might be decided that without specialist staff it would not be possible to meet the particular care needs of a young homeless person who suffers from schizophrenia. Alternatively it might be decided that the organisation can meet their need for temporary accommodation if the specialist care needs are met by another agency, e.g. community psychiatric nursing service.

Standards

Having actively listened to the expressed needs and expectations of the key stakeholders (beneficiaries, funders etc.) and agreed which of them the organisation is willing and able (perhaps with some planning and effort) to meet, it should now be possible to start the process of compiling a list of key standards for the services that the organisation is providing or is planning to provide. Put another way, these standards represent what the organisation is prepared to promise to its stakeholders, particularly to the beneficiaries.

Moments of truth

One way of thinking about the different aspects of an organisation's work that are likely to have a significant impact on its beneficiaries is to think of the user's journey or pathway through the organisation, i.e. the complete sequence of contact that an individual beneficiary has with the organisation. These points of contact are sometimes called 'moments of truth'. It is useful to consider what the main activities are that will affect how well (or badly) the needs and expectations of the individual will be met at those moments of truth. It can be useful to try and draw the sequence as a diagram. For example, in an advice agency the key sequence might be as shown in Figure 4.1. It is very likely that how an individual assesses the quality of the advice agency will largely depend on how these three key moments of truth or points of interface are dealt with. Significantly the first of the contacts is likely to be with a receptionist, not a professional advisor, so as is often the case, the receptionist plays an important role in the perception of quality in an organisation.

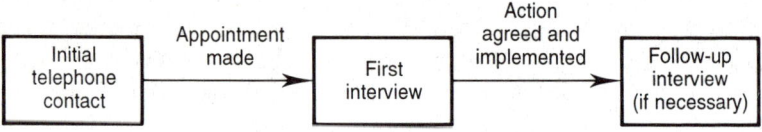

Figure 4.1 Advice agency – moments of truth.

The standards that are likely to be developed for this advice agency would certainly include how initial phone calls seeking advice are handled; how individuals are received and dealt with when they arrive on the premises, and how initial and any follow-up interviews are conducted by the advisor.

Øvretveit (1994) argues that this mapping process has a number of advantages in creating quality improvement:

First, a simple description in itself suggests changes that would improve quality. If the process cannot be described because it is too complex, or because staff cannot agree what happens, then there are bound to be quality problems. Second, staff can generate lists of quality problems for each stage and prioritise the lists to decide which problems to work on, using conventional quality methods or a conventional audit cycle.

One of the main advantages of staff using this approach is that they can work together as a team to describe what happens, learning about how the work situation and its organisation will cause quality problems.

This kind of model lends itself well to the 'mystery shopper' technique of evaluating a service by getting a number of people to present themselves to the agency with a relevant problem or need and to assess how they are treated at each stage of the process and then to feed back this customer-eyed view of the quality of your services. This can be disturbingly revealing!

Often the sequence of activities will be more complicated than the simple model above. For example, a hostel or residential home might develop a model which looks more like Figure 4.2.

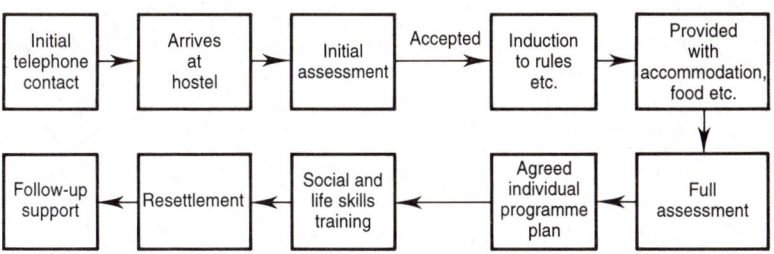

Figure 4.2 Hostel/home – moments of truth.

To ensure the needs of the individual are met, standards would need to be developed for each stage of this process.

The expectations of the beneficiaries or potential beneficiaries of the services are likely to fall into three main categories:

- Core product or service;
- Physical surroundings;
- Customer care.

For each of these main categories the Local Government Management Board have suggested that there are a number of important questions that can be asked which can help to clarify the quality of the service:

The core product or service

- What are the purposes of the service?
- Does it meet those purposes?
- Who are the users of the service, for which it is designed?
- Does the service reach those users?
- Does it meet the requirements of those users?
- Is the service reliable and free from faults?
- Is the service timely, delivered at the most effective time?
- Does the service have any unintended ill-effects?
- Does the user have adequate redress in case of failure?

The physical surroundings

- How do the surroundings in which the service is delivered affect its quality?
- What are the important aspects of the service surroundings?
- Do the service surroundings enhance or diminish the quality of the service?
- Are the physical aspects of the surroundings relevant to the quality of service?
- Are the social circumstances in which the service is delivered relevant to the quality of service?
- How are staff affected by the surroundings in which they work?

Customer care

- Is there a direct relationship between those providing the service and those using the service?
- How will people be feeling when they use the service?
- How do users value the service relationship?
- How are staff affected by the service relationship?
- Is the relationship welcoming, supportive and responsive?
- Are both user and provider aware of the demands of the service relationship?
- Does information, explanation and understanding meet the requirements of the users?
- How can staff be helped to develop good relationships with users?
- How do those who do not meet the users contribute to the service relationship?

These questions are adapted from *The Quality Question* by Stewart and Walsh (1989).

Box 4.4

There are pitfalls to be avoided in the development of standards:

Box 4.4 *continued*

1. It is important to keep in mind that it is the totality of what the beneficiary experiences that impacts on their perception of the quality of the service. It is often apparently minor and unintended items that can have the biggest impact, positively and negatively. For example, if someone goes into a shop and buys an attractive bunch of flowers at a reasonable price, isn't kept waiting, and the sales person is courteous and efficient, the person is likely to feel satisfied, but if the floor is very slippery and the person falls and bangs their head on the corner of a shelf, their feeling of satisfaction is likely to rapidly disappear!
2. It is also useful to be aware that what everyone really wants is not just to have their expectations met, but to have them exceeded: we want more than an acceptable service, we'd really like exceptional service – we want to be delighted! The danger in creating minimum standards is that they easily become maximum standards, too, and staff make no effort to do better than the minimum written standard. It is important to create a culture that not only aims to meet expectations but to exceed them and encourages staff to want to provide exceptional service, and delight the organisation's beneficiaries.
3. The needs of individuals are all different. The establishment of standards should be aimed at facilitating the meeting of the particular needs of each individual and not inhibiting them by establishing a uniform service for everyone.
4. And last, but not least, is the danger of creating static standards when the needs and expectations of people are constantly changing (normally increasing). It is vital to view quality management in an organisation as a process of continuous improvement, to regularly review the standards with the stakeholders, discussed earlier, and constantly looking at ways of better meeting their needs and expectations.

Internal customers

The above discussion has tried to clarify the meaning of quality for voluntary organisations and to suggest a process for drawing up quality standards or outcomes for the key areas of work that will have an impact on the needs and expectations of the beneficiary. It is also important to look at how these standards might be achieved. But before moving on to how to assure quality, it is vital not to ignore the needs of the *internal customer*, which is an important quality concept.

Not everyone in an organisation carries out activities which impact directly on the beneficiaries, although they might be absolutely vital, indirectly, or in the longer-term, in meeting their needs. There may be trustees, staff or volunteers who have virtually no contact with the beneficiaries. Does this mean they have no role in a quality initiative? Certainly not! They are likely to have an important role in supplying services (or products) to others who deal directly with the beneficiaries. The internal supplier-customer chain may be even longer before there is a direct impact on the beneficiaries.

Everyone in an organisation is both a customer and a supplier to other individuals (staff and volunteers) within the organisation. They might provide training or supervision (as a supplier) to the staff, or be trained or supervised (customer); they might do the typing or photocopying (supplier) or ask for a publication to be ordered (customer).

These internal supplier-customer interfaces are vital in an organisation and often operate across normal department divisions where these exist (especially in large organisations). It is very important that, as internal customers, each person is clear about what is expected of other staff/volunteers in their role as internal suppliers. Unlike the situation with external customers, where, if there is a dissatisfaction with a particular service or product it is normally the fault of the supplier, perhaps in not producing what was required, or not delivering on time, etc., with the internal supplier-customer chain at least an equal responsibility needs to be on the customer to be clear and specific about what they need and expect, and then to come to an agreement on the extent that the internal supplier is willing and able to meet those needs and expectations.

Clarifying the role of support services such as personnel, training and finance as suppliers of crucial services to internal customers is an important area in any organisation. It can be a significant source of conflict when support services are perceived by the operational parts of the organisation (e.g. those providing a service to the public) as a *customer* making continual and unreasonable demands on other parts of the organisation, rather than as a *supplier* of consultancy and advice services to help managers and staff within the organisation to do their job better.

Organisational model

The focus on the needs of beneficiaries and the concept of internal customers and suppliers leads to a very different model of an organisation than the traditional hierarchical staff chart. The quality organisational model might look more like Figure 4.3.

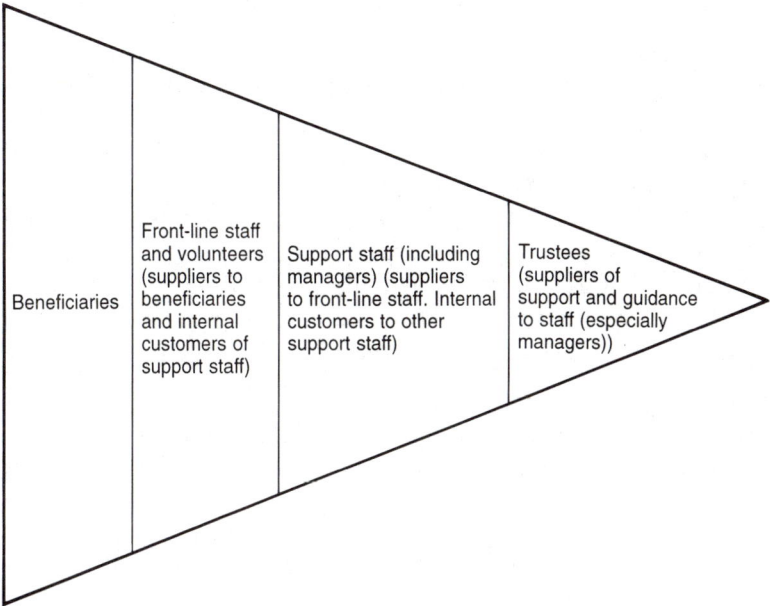

Figure 4.3 Organisational model (from a quality perspective).

Quality assurance

Having agreed the standards to be achieved, how can an organisation make sure that these standards are indeed achieved and achieved consistently?

A traditional answer to this question might have been that from time to time, the trustees of the organisation (or more likely its funders) would carry out, or commission, an inspection or evaluation and produce a report on where the service fell below the standards expected by the inspectors, and then hope the faults will be rectified. This approach should not be dismissed as it can be one useful tool in assessing quality and making improvements. However, it does have significant limitations which are highlighted by some of the key principles of the quality movement.

1. The fundamental importance of focusing on the beneficiaries, which suggests that whatever it is that ensures the quality of a service must have the views of those beneficiaries at its heart.
2. The fundamental belief that prevention is central to quality assurance and is much more effective than inspection at the end of a process. Therefore systems to establish and maintain quality need to be built into all aspects of the service, from the supply of resources, through the activity itself to the final outcome and any follow-up.
3. The belief that it is everyone's responsibility to ensure quality not just inspectors, or quality managers, etc.
4. The belief that there needs to be a commitment to a process of continuous improvement and not just improvements as a result of occasional inspections or evaluations.

Quality management implies building in quality assurance at all levels throughout an organisation, so that the likelihood of mistakes or failures in meeting the agreed needs of beneficiaries is very small. Indeed the target which is constantly aimed for is no mistakes, failures or waste at all. A common model of the work of an organisation which can be very helpful in thinking about quality looks something like Figure 4.4.

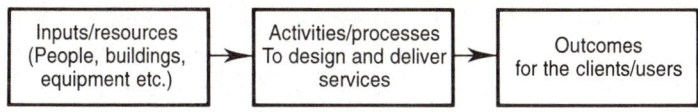

Figure 4.4 Process model.

Quality systems

If the final outcomes for the beneficiaries are 'to satisfy' their 'agreed needs', then it is necessary to establish systems that ensure that *inputs of resources* are of the necessary standard. It is also vital that the whole range of *activities or processes* that take place to determine and deliver the services to the beneficiaries are also controlled by a comprehensive quality management or assurance system. Quality assurance has been defined as:

> all those planned and systematic actions necessary to provide adequate confidence that a product or service will satisfy given requirements for quality. (British Standard (BS) 4778)

The key question is how does an organisation start establishing such a quality assurance management system?

Having established the standards that the organisation intends to achieve consistently, it is necessary to look at the work that the trustees and each of the staff and volunteers do, and draw up procedures for those key activities which may affect whether the agreed standards will be achieved or not.

What these procedures are, like the standards themselves, will be different for each individual organisation, but when looked at together they should cover all the main activities/processes which have an impact on meeting the needs of the beneficiaries.

Ideally these procedures should initially be drafted by the people who do the relevant jobs themselves rather than the trustees, managers or a consultant, although this initial draft may need to be amended. The procedures should make it clear to somebody who knows nothing about the job: what the purpose and scope of the procedure is; what the key stages in the specific procedure are; whose responsibility it is to carry out each stage; and how it is recorded that the procedure has been carried out properly. An example of a procedure is given in Box 4.5.

There also needs to be a system that ensures that the appropriate person is alerted when an agreed procedure is not properly followed; so that action to rectify the situation is taken and consideration is given as to how it can be ensured that the problem does not recur. This might be through training, revising the procedure, etc.

There needs to be a system that ensures that the standards and procedures are regularly reviewed and improved, taking on board the views and continuously changing needs and expectations of the beneficiaries.

All the above can be seen as simply good management practice for an organisation and will incorporate many things that most organisations will already be doing, but perhaps in not such a systematic and comprehensive way as is suggested here. It is not a fad that will soon go away, but a necessary process for all voluntary organisations in responding to rapidly changing needs and increased demands for greater accountability.

Box 4.5

Referral procedure for Springboard Hostel

1. The referral is to be treated in a friendly and courteous manner at all times.
2. Where possible/appropriate the referral is accompanied by a member of project staff throughout the interview process.
3. Explain the referral procedure and policy to the potential resident (the referral policy is found in the policy manual).
4. If the referral does not meet the criteria in the referral policy, or there is no bed available, explain reasons and where possible source alternative accommodation.
5. If the potential resident meets the criteria in the referral policy:
    (a) Confirm acceptance with resident, subject to approval of project leader.

Box 4.5 *continued*

 (b) Complete the resident admissions form and sign (ensure the resident signs the form).
 (c) Supply resident with information pack.
 (d) Complete Housing Benefit and Income Support Forms (where appropriate) and forward to Housing Department and Social Security Agency respectively.
 (e) Ensure referral book and daily diary are completed.
 (f) Send statistics sheet (on monthly basis) to information department.
 (g) Open resident file and insert admissions form.
 (h) Outline services provided.
 (i) Show resident to accommodation and explain contents of Health and Safety check-list.

Responsibility: Any project staff member.

Quality problems

Even having carried out all of the processes described above there will still be problems that need to be overcome. These problems are likely to fall into a number of different categories depending on where in the process they take place. Figure 4.5 shows a model which can be useful in identifying which category of problem you might be trying to deal with.

External recognition

One of the questions that some voluntary organisations are currently grappling with is whether it is helpful or necessary to introduce an *externally assessed* quality assurance system such as BS EN ISO 9000 (known formerly as BS5750 in the UK). This standard was originally developed in the defence industry to improve the consistency of the quality standards of mortar shells!

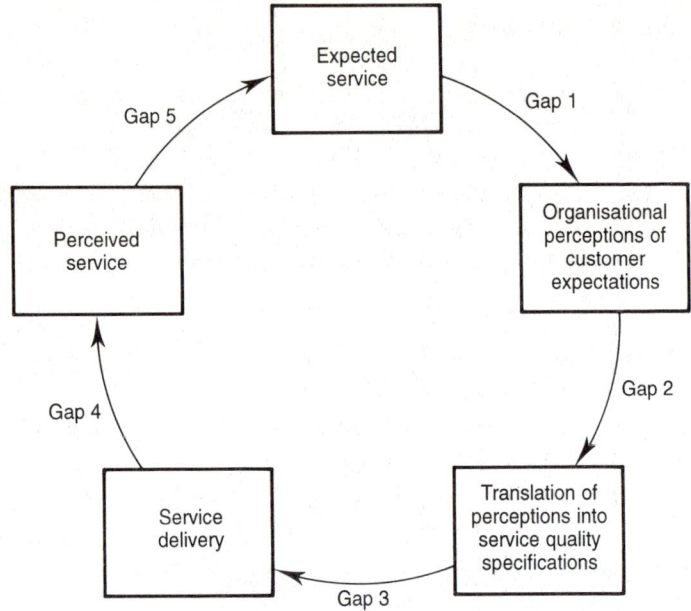

Figure 4.5 Gap diagnosis model (adapted from Zeithaml *et al* 1985). This model is useful in identifying a number of different types of quality problems that can occur.
Gap 1: A gap here suggests that there is a significant difference between what the beneficiaries really want and what the organisation thinks they want. This often occurs simply because they are not asked, or not asked regularly or because of their negative life experiences they don't feel confident enough to express their real wishes.
Gap 2: This occurs because the quality standards and procedures established are not sufficient to actually ensure the expected service is delivered and delivered consistently.
Gap 3: In this situation the standards and procedures might be right but the staff and volunteers who have to deliver them may not have been adequately trained to carry them out properly.
Gap 4: This is known as the 'marketing gap' where an organisation is taken in by its own PR, but can't deliver what it promised in its marketing of the service.
Gap 5: This is the key gap between what the customer expected and what he/she perceived that he/she actually received. Problems can occur at any or all of these points and need to be tackled appropriately.

This is not a promising start for a system that may be of use to the voluntary sector.

Reading the standard itself is likely to confirm for the voluntary sector reader that it is not for them, as the wording is very manufacturing orientated (see Box 4.6). But underneath the off-putting wording is really a simple idea of a type of system that any organisation should have if it is to stand over the quality of the services or products it provides. It is also consistent with the suggestions earlier in this chapter about the development of clear accountable procedures.

The main clauses of BS EN ISO 9000 are contained in Box 4.6.

Box 4.6

BS EN ISO 9000: Main clauses

Quality System Requirements
1. Management responsibility
2. Quality system
3. Contract review
4. Design control
5. Document and data control
6. Purchasing
7. Control of customer – supplied product
8. Product identification and traceability
9. Process control
10. Inspection and testing
11. Control of inspection, measuring and test equipment
12. Inspection and test staters
13. Control of non-conforming products
14. Corrective and preventive action
15. Handling, storage, packaging, preservation and delivery
16. Control of quality records
17. Internal quality audits
18. Training
19. Servicing
20. Statistical techniques

Main elements of BS EN ISO 9000

In essence BS EN ISO 9000 involves the following:
- Establishing a quality programme and policy;
- Training all staff in quality policy and procedures;
- Designing the organisation to maximise quality;
- Ensuring the responsibilities for quality are clear;
- Developing sampling, testing and inspection procedures, where necessary;
- Purchasing quality inputs (including sampling, testing and inspection of bought-in products);
- Planning output;
- Developing appropriate production/service delivery methods;
- Monitoring work in progress;
- Ensuring quality control of output;
- Corrective action;
- Creating a documentary record system that enables quality to be managed;
- Systems for identifying work and materials at each point;
- Document control;
- Handling, storage, packing and delivery of products;
- Building in traceability of work;
- Control of non-conforming products;
- Auditing the quality system.

With some adaptation most of the above are applicable to the voluntary sector.

Motives

Many people in the voluntary sector are sceptical about the relevance or appropriateness of BS EN ISO 9000 to their work. Part of the difficulty has been that like many new ideas it has been oversold. Many people know companies who have introduced BS EN ISO 9000 and have been awarded a quality mark, but the quality of the company's services or products has remained poor or erratic. The reason for this is twofold.

Many companies have introduced BS EN ISO 9000 for the

wrong reason. They want to be able to compete better for business and feel that a quality mark on their note paper will improve their image and competitiveness. Many companies and other purchasers are now looking for their suppliers to have BS EN ISO 9000 as well. Companies also like to be able to say they are a 'quality company', but there is often no real commitment to continuous improvement, or to being orientated towards the needs and expectations of the customer.

Secondly, BS EN ISO 9000 does not itself stipulate what standards an organisation should try and meet, but only provides a management framework within which the standards the organisation sets can be achieved consistently. The standards set may be perceived as 'poor quality' by the customer, BS EN ISO 9000 or not.

However, as part of an overall quality improvement programme the introduction of BS EN ISO 9000 can be helpful, and introduces the discipline of external assessment to ensure that the organisation is doing consistently what it says it is doing. See the case study on pages 94 and 95 of a housing association that introduced BS EN ISO 9000 (BS5750 as it was called in the UK until recently.)

Disadvantages

There are other criticisms of BS EN ISO 9000 which need to be considered when thinking about whether it might be appropriate for a particular organisation.

1. BS EN ISO 9000 is often seen as a bureaucratic, paper-driven system, which is anathema to many in the voluntary sector. Indeed BS EN ISO 9000 does require a certain level of controlled systems and procedures and tight document control. However some of these systems may already exist in the organisation and BS EN ISO 9000 should tighten up their use so that they are more effective. It is probably one of the important skills when introducing BS EN ISO 9000 to ensure that old systems and procedures are discarded when the new ones are introduced, and that the new or revised systems and procedures are as clear, concise and relevant as possible.

94   Quality assurance and management

2. BS EN ISO 9000 is seen as expensive. In addition to the costs involved in external assessment there are now large numbers of quality consultants who are peddling their wares round any companies or organisations who show some interest in quality assurance. Some of them are very expensive and they may well not be the right consultants for a voluntary organisation. However, it is very likely that most organisations will need some form of experienced external support (around 15 days consultancy time is common). Ensure that a number of different consultants are talked to. Ensure that the consultant has a feel for the voluntary sector, has a real commitment to improving quality in the organisation, and is competitive in terms of price (many will negotiate a lower fee for a voluntary organisation).

Case study Belfast Improved Houses

Belfast Improved Houses Limited is the second largest Housing Association in Northern Ireland, with over 2,000 units located in the Greater Belfast area and beyond. Established twenty years ago primarily to rehabilitate older terraced housing in the inner city, the Association now provides all types of accommodation for a wide range of client groups.

In 1991 the Association made a decision to seek BS5750 accreditation as the framework for managing change within the organisation's internal and external environment. The growing size and geographical spread of the Association has meant not only an increase in the number of staff but, in the case of residential staff, in their location. They felt that the introduction of BS5750 would ensure that each member of staff had a uniform approach to their job and would create a greater organisational awareness by improving communications with and within the residential staff.

The Association also recognised the changing nature of the voluntary housing movement and the requirements placed on it by Government. The introduction of 'mixed' funding in place of 100% grants was occurring and it was important that the Association actively sought to preserve and indeed, enhance its market position. They felt that the awarding of BS5750 would place the Association ahead of all others in the province.

A leading local firm of management consultants were appointed to oversee the introduction of BS5750 to the Association. They briefed the steering group (management team) on the appointment of a quality manager (the Director of Housing) and a quality circle of five members appointed by each of the quality action teams (QATs) representing the different departments within the Association, i.e. Development, Housing Management, Finance, Resident Wardens and Resident Supervisors.

The QATs met weekly from April 1992 to commence the lengthy exercise of writing procedures to cover the main aspect of their job. These procedures were then approved by the quality circle before being ratified by the steering group. Each QAT produced a manual of procedures which were also incorporated in the quality manual written by the Director of Housing.

A quality noticeboard was established in the main office to bring information and progress to all members of staff. The Association's quality policy signed by the management team was displayed in all advice centres, sheltered dwellings and blocks of supervised flats to demonstrate to staff and tenants alike of the commitment towards quality.

The writing of procedures and preparing the Association for an initial accreditation visit took over eighteen months. In all, over eighty procedures were written by the QATs. As part of the system, quality auditors had to be trained by a qualified BS5750 auditor in order to enable the Association to audit its own procedures and demonstrate that its systems were regularly examined and reviewed. The steering group (management team) also met six-monthly to review performance and identify trends.

In March 1993 an application was made to the accreditation body to request an audit later in the year. Before this audit took place in September 1993 a mock audit was undertaken by the management consultancy to look at those key areas which would be scrutinised at the time of audit.

The eventual accreditation audit took a day and the Association was awarded BS5750 Part 2, 1987 on 15 September 1993.

The process however did not end there. Accreditation audits take place every six months and a major non-compliance discovered can result in the certificate being withdrawn if corrective action is not in place by the time of the following audit. In-house audits have also continued. These are seen as essential for two reasons; to demonstrate to external auditors that the system is continually under scrutiny and also to show up problems that may be occurring. The QATs continue to meet on a regular basis to examine their own procedures to see that these continue to be the best way to do things.

The Association feel it has benefited from the awarding of BS5750 not only from the resultant publicity and 'grapevine' effect but significantly, in staff relations and in the service to our tenants.

Quality costs

When considering the cost of introducing BS EN ISO 9000 it is necessary to consider this against the current cost of quality in the organisation. These costs might include:

- The costs involved in repeating work that was done incorrectly before;
- The costs involved in dealing with mistakes;
- Loss of support, perhaps from donors or statutory funders/purchasers;
- The costs involved in closely monitoring/inspecting work to catch mistakes before they do any damage;
- Damaged public image and the cost of trying to repair it;
- The damage caused to beneficiaries who do not get the service they need.

So although there is some truth in the above concerns, they do not necessarily mean that BS EN ISO 9000 is not a valuable tool for some voluntary organisations in trying to ensure the consistency and quality of services provided.

Tom Peters, a leading writer on management issues has said:

> Most total quality programmes fail for one of two reasons: they have passion but no system, or system without passion.

This section so far has been about creating the systems, we now move on to the 'passion'.

Continuous improvement

Quality is not something that has an end or completion point, it is a 'race without an end'. However, one of the dangers of a quality assurance system such as BS EN ISO 9000 is that once it has been introduced and awarded, everybody feels that they can sit back and quality will happen. It can be disappointing to find out that it won't. In addition to systems, there needs to be created a culture or climate of continuous improvement from the top to the bottom of the organisation (as well as from side-to-side) which has the full and active support of the trustees and senior staff.

To be effective, everyone (trustees, staff, and volunteers, committee members) must feel that quality is their responsibility and that they each have a crucial role to play in continually improving the organisation's ability to meet the needs and expectations of the beneficiaries. This will not work in an organisation where there is an atmosphere of fear, and staff are afraid to speak out and are not allowed to be involved in discussions about their work.

In a total quality philosophy, problems are not caused by individuals, but by the failure of systems. The only solution to quality problems is to understand what you are trying to do and clarify what is the best way of achieving that objective consistently. Valerie Stewart in *The David Solution* (1990) tells the story that:

> Michelangelo was asked how he managed to create his statue of David from its original marble block. 'It was easy' he is said to have replied. 'I just chipped away the bits that weren't David.'

In the same way, in tackling quality problems it should be

possible to empower individuals to identify and remove the blockages to achieving the agreed standards. Everything in an organisation that does not contribute to meeting the needs of the beneficiaries is waste and should be 'chipped away'.

Continuous improvement is also not primarily an individualistic process, but one that should be developed on a team-work basis. Throughout the organisation each individual should have the opportunity to meet with others as part of a team on a regular basis simply to discuss how things could be done better, i.e. how the needs and expectations of beneficiaries and other stakeholders (internal as well as external) can be satisfied. These are sometimes called quality circles or quality improvement teams.

Creating a quality culture

So how can this culture of continuous improvement be developed? There is a range of initiatives that can be taken. What will be appropriate may be different in different organisations, but might include:

1. Regular staff/volunteer attitude surveys are carried out to establish where the organisation is at the moment in creating a quality 'culture' and help identify what needs to be done to bring about progress.
2. The organisation's mission/vision statement (discussed in Chapter 2) is written or revised to reflect the centrality of meeting the needs of the clients/users/customers and a process of continuous improvement.
3. An organisational statement of values/principles (discussed in Chapter 2) is developed or revised to reflect both the commitment to the valuing and empowerment of staff and volunteers and most importantly the focus on the beneficiaries and commitment to continuous improvement.
4. All staff are made aware of these commitments. This awareness can be tested by the regular attitude surveys suggested in (1) above.
5. Training is organised for all trustees, staff and volunteers in the principles of total quality management in a voluntary sector context (including customer care).

6. Quality concepts and standards are written into job descriptions and person specifications.
7. All trustees, staff and volunteers are allocated to a team and asked to come up with recommendations for improving the quality of the work of their particular project or unit.
8. Special working groups of trustees, staff and volunteers are established to take forward specific recommendations from these quality improvement meetings.
9. Improvements introduced, (even small ones) are publicised and celebrated.

Assessment

A total quality programme is not as easy to define or assess as a quality assurance system like BS EN ISO 9000 (it is much more about changing the culture of an organisation), but there are various characteristics that organisations with a high level of commitment to total quality management tend to share. The British Quality Foundation has developed a UK Quality Award to give recognition to organisations who have taken a lead in this area. From their experience of assessing organisations for this award they have developed a self-assessment guide which can be helpful to individual organisations in developing a total quality approach.

The suggested areas to address in the self-assessment guide fall into two groups.

1. Enablers: which are those factors which are concerned with the organisation's approach to total quality;
2. Results: which are about what the organisation has achieved and is achieving.

The suggested key areas to address follow.

Enablers

1. Leadership: the behaviour of all managers in driving the organisation towards total quality.

2. Policy and strategy: the organisation's mission, values, vision and strategic direction and the manner in which it achieves them.
3. People management: the management of the organisation's people.
4. Resources: the management, utilisation and preservation of resources.
5. Processes: the management of all value-added activities within the organisation.

Results

6. Customer satisfaction: what the perception of external customers is of the organisation and of its products and services.
7. People (i.e. staff satisfaction): what your people's feelings are about their organisation.
8. Impact on society: what the perception of the organisation is amongst the community at large.
9. Organisational: what the organisation is achieving in relation to its planned performance.

(from 'Guide to Self Assessment' British Quality Foundation).

Some 'key excellence indicators' for each area are included in Appendix 1.

As can be seen from the above lists, total quality management involves a wide range of areas throughout an organisation (hence the word 'total'). It is also very consistent with both the strategic planning model explored earlier and the development of quality people to be dealt with in the next chapter.

Key points

The quality of the services and the other activities provided by voluntary organisations is crucial to the development of the sector, in meeting the real needs and aspirations of those it exists to serve, and in providing greater accountability to funding bodies and the public. Success in ensuring this quality requires a number of key elements:

- A real commitment to put beneficiaries first.
- A strategy of 'active listening' to the beneficiaries.
- Clear, comprehensive and assessable standards for the services we provide.
- Procedures for ensuring that standards are met consistently.
- Procedures for corrective action when standards are not met.
- Training for all trustees, staff and volunteers in quality.
- A commitment to continuous improvement throughout the organisation starting from the top.
- The opportunity for individuals to be part of a team who can put forward suggestions for improvement.

5 Quality people

An organisation is known by the people it keeps.

Chapter summary

The life blood of a voluntary organisation is its people. Only if the trustees, staff and volunteers have the appropriate skills and knowledge can they effectively achieve the organisation's aims and objectives. This chapter highlights a competence-based approach to the recruitment and development of staff and volunteers. National vocational qualifications (NVQs) provide ready-made competency standards for many jobs in the voluntary sector. The framework for NVQs in Care is used as an example to illustrate the structure of NVQs. The 'Investors in people' award framework is highlighted as it helps organisations link strategic planning to analysing and addressing the training and development needs of their people. It also stresses the importance of properly evaluating training. The chapter also concludes with two short case studies of organisations that have used the 'Investors in people' framework along with development of NVQs.

Competency approach

The chapters so far have looked at how to draw up, implement and review plans to tackle the kinds of urgent needs and issues that voluntary organisations are concerned with, and to ensure the quality of services and products provided to beneficiaries, by establishing quality standards and procedures, and by creating a culture of continuous improvement. All of these will come to nothing, however, if the people (trustees, staff and volunteers) who will have to carry all this through don't have the necessary skills, knowledge or aptitudes. Despite this, evidence from the Industrial Society shows that spending on training in the UK is among the lowest in Europe at 3.28% of the salary bill, and is even lower in the public/voluntary sector (at 2.84% of the salary bill).

This chapter considers how voluntary organisations can ensure the quality of their staff and volunteers. To do this requires a number of key steps, which can be summarised as follows:

1. Clarify the roles (i.e. the job) of each trustee, member of staff and volunteer in terms of results (or outputs) including the contribution that they are expected to make towards achieving the aims and quality standards of the organisation.
2. Clarify the skills, knowledge and aptitudes (i.e. inputs) that are required to carry out each of these roles successfully.
3. Use (1) and (2) above to recruit and select new trustees, staff, and volunteers;
4. Use (1) and (2) above as bench marks to appraise trustees, staff, and volunteers and to assess the training/development needs of each individual and team (including the management/executive committee);
5. Use (1), (2) and (4) to plan and implement a programme of training and development for trustees, staff and volunteers as individuals and teams;
6. Evaluate the impact of the training and repeat (4).

A model of this process might look something like Figure 5.1. Experience would suggest that carrying out this simple looking model involves a very significant amount of time, thought and effort, but that can pay significant dividends.

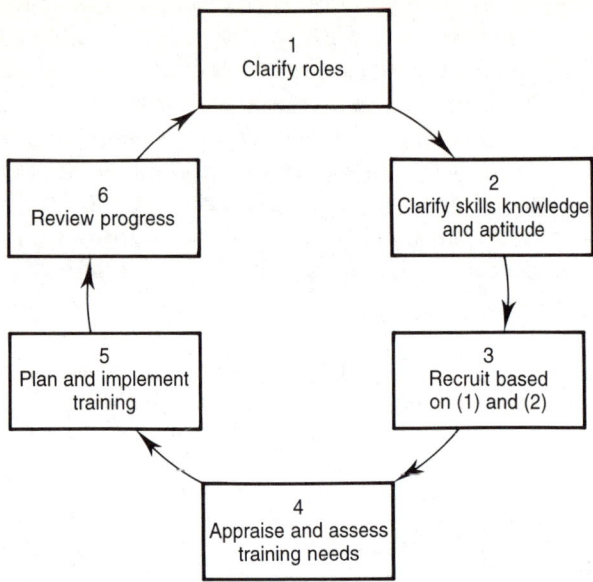

Figure 5.1 Model for ensuring quality people.

National competency frameworks

Help is also at hand because a substantial amount of work has already been done to analyse many kinds of jobs in order to establish NVQs, which enable on-the-job skills and knowledge to be accredited. For most jobs in the voluntary sector there will be a relevant NVQ which provides a detailed breakdown of a similar job role and specifies what standards will need to be achieved to carry out the job proficiently. Of course, the fit between a particular NVQ and any particular job in the voluntary sector will not be perfect, but the voluntary sector has played an important role in drawing up and piloting many of the standards, so the standards should at least to some extent reflect the ethos of the voluntary sector. These national standards can be tremendously valuable in helping to analyse a particular job and clarifying the skills, knowledge and aptitude required to do that job.

It can be helpful however, to try and customise (i.e. re-word and perhaps re-structure) the relevant national standards where this will make them more easily understandable and more clearly relevant to the appropriate people in the organisation.

Relevant national standards

Some of the national standards currently available that are of particular interest to the voluntary sector include:

- Care
- Childcare and education
- Housing
- Criminal justice
- Advice, guidance and counselling
- Management
- Business administration
- Personnel
- Training and development
- Retail (particularly for those organisations with charity shops)
- Playwork
- Sport and recreation
- Health care
- Public relations
- Environmental conservation
- Information and library service
- Direct marketing
- Cultural venues (forthcoming)
- Family care and education (forthcoming)
- Community work (forthcoming)
- Special needs housing (forthcoming)
- Sensory deprivation (forthcoming)

but there may be many others that might have particular significance to one or more roles within any particular organisation, and there are many others that are in the process of being established.

A full list of current and planned national standards is available from the National Council for Vocational Qualifications (NCVQ).

Structure of national standards

For those not familiar with the structure of national standards, or NVQs, the example of the National standards in CARE can provide a useful indication of the kind of format and content of the standard. These were developed to be relevant to a wide range of social care staff in both residential and day care settings.

National standards may be established at up to five different levels from 1 to 5 depending on the complexity of the role. However, the standards in care are currently only available at two levels (2 and 3). Level 3 is relevant to jobs of greater complexity and responsibility than those relevant to Level 2.

In both levels of the care standards there is a compulsory value base unit entitled 'Promote equality for all individuals'. This contains five elements which the lead body believes should underpin all work in the social care sector and are very familiar to those working in the voluntary sector. The elements of the value base unit relate closely to the kind of statement of values/principles that were discussed in Chapter 2. These core value elements are as follows:

- Promote anti-discriminatory practice;
- Maintain the confidentiality of information;
- Promote and support individual rights and choice within service delivery;
- Acknowledge individual's personal beliefs and identity;
- Support individuals through effective communication.

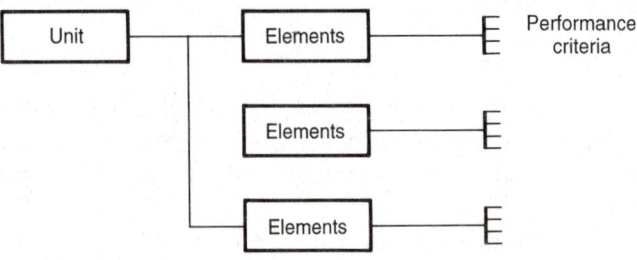

Figure 5.2 NVQ structure of national standards.

Structure of national standards

Like all national standards, these elements, which all care workers are expected to be able to carry out competently, are further broken down into detailed 'performance criteria' which define the relevant behaviours expected for each element. There are also 'range statements' which indicate the range of situations in which someone should be able to demonstrate the relevant skill.

In addition to the core value base unit, Level 2 of the national standards in care has five further core units regardless of what part of the care sector the organisation or individual might be in or the type of beneficiary. These core units are as follows:

1. Contribute to the protection of individuals from abuse;
2. Contribute to the ongoing support of clients and others significant to them;
3. Support clients in transition due to their care requirements;
4. Contribute to the health, safety and security of individuals and their environment;
5. Obtain, transmit and store information relating to the delivery of a care service.

As in all NVQ units, these core units are, in turn, broken down into their respective elements. For example the unit 'contribute to the protection of individuals from abuse' is broken down into three elements:

- Contribute to minimising the level of abuse in a care environment;
- Challenge disruptive or abusive behaviour;
- Contribute to monitoring individuals who are at risk from abuse.

For level 3 of the national standards in care, there are a number of additional compulsory core units. These are as follows:

- Contribute to the management of aggressive and abusive behaviour;
- Promote communication with clients where there are communication difficulties;
- Support clients when they are distressed;
- Enable clients to make use of available services and information.

These are also broken down into their respective elements, performance criteria and range indicators. An example of one element from NVQs in care is included as Box 5.1.

Box 5.1

Unit 23 Contribute to the management of aggressive and abusive behaviour

Element

23a Contribute to the promotion of non-aggressive and non-abusive behaviour

Performance criteria

23.a.1 the client's behaviour pattern is identified and used to promote less aggressive or abusive behaviour in a manner which is consistent with the client's individuality and personal beliefs and preferences (Oa2, 3, 4, 5; Oc4; Oel, 2)

23.a.2 the client's plan of care is implemented accurately and consistently (Oa7; Oc10; Oe3)

23.a.3 the boundaries of acceptable behaviour are agreed with the client of her/his representative and the consequences of breaking them explained in a manner, and at a level and pace, appropriate to her/him (Od5; Oe9)

23.a.4 preventive action taken is agreed with the care team and is appropriate to known specific factors which trigger or provoke aggression or abuse

23.a.5 the client is supported in activities which are likely to stimulate her/his interest and are consistent with her/his preference

23.a.6 where behaviour is likely to lead to aggression or abuse, action appropriate to the client, her/his behaviour and condition is initiated with minimum possible delay (Oc5,7)

Box 5.1 *continued*

23.a.7 where aggression or abuse is expressed or demonstrated, this is responded to in a manner which acknowledges the expression whilst taking account of personal safety (Oc4)

23.a.8 approaches to the client are carried out in a manner which is likely to be perceived as non-threatening and are consistent with any legal and organisational constraints (Oc8)

23.a.9 where further assistance is required, it is called without delay (Od7; Oe1)

23.a.10 the client is supported to find alternative ways of expressing her/his feelings which are consistent with the agreed approach, the plan of care and demonstrate less aggression or abuse (Oc3, 8)

Range

Aggressive/abusive behaviour: a) through communication (verbal and non verbal) 2) physical.

Behaviour directed at: 1) self 2) others 3) the material environment.

Legislation/organisational policies relating to: 1) all individuals 2) specific care settings or clients (such as the Mental Health Act).

The worker's practice is consistent with her/his occupations role and is under the supervision, direction or guidance of an appropriate person(s) accountable in the relevant area of practice.

(Crown Copyright 1992. Produced by the Care Sector Consortium.)

Endorsements

In addition to the compulsory core units and elements there are also standards (units, elements and performance criteria) established for different types of workers within the care sector. These are known as endorsements and for an individual to be awarded a full NVQ, he or she would need to demonstrate competence in all the units within the most relevant endorsement (between four and six units within each endorsement) as well as the compulsory core units. The current optional endorsements include the following:

Level 2 Developmental care
Direct care
Domiciliary care
Residential/hospital support
Post-natal care
Special care needs
Combined support
Independent living support
Activity and access support

Level 3 Promoting independence
Supported living
Rehabilitative care
Continuing care
Supportive long-term care
Terminal care
Acute care
Acute care (children)
Clinic and out-patient care
Substance use
Support and protection
Self and environmental management skills
Mental health care
Mobility and movement
Foot care
Communication

Going through the units and elements in each endorsement will provide a good indication of which endorsements might be relevant to the care staff in a particular organisation, if any.

It is useful to ask a group of staff or volunteers doing similar jobs within the organisation to simply indicate against each element in the relevant standards whether they feel that it is something that is relevant to their job. Those that are not can be set aside, unless the person wishes to proceed towards achieving an NVQ.

Contextualisation

For those elements that remain it is likely that some of the wording will feel strange or inappropriate for any particular organisation. The group members may suggest alternative wordings that provide a better 'fit' without creating a totally different meaning. If this exercise is done for each of the elements, performance indicators and range statements a very detailed statement of standards of competence, that individuals within the organisation should have or develop, can be established.

Uses

Experience indicates that where organisations have gone through this process the standards have been very useful for:

1. Drawing up and/or reviewing job descriptions, which can be revised to follow the structure and much of the content of the NVQ units and elements.
2. Drawing up and/or reviewing person specifications, i.e. the desirable characteristics of candidates to fill vacant posts.
3. Assessing the current capabilities of existing staff/volunteers at an appraisal or performance review (as an individual or team exercise) against the standards (see Chapter 3).
4. Establishing the training needs of existing staff and volunteers.
5. Drawing up training and development plans for individuals and groups of staff and volunteers to meet the training needs identified.
6. Enabling staff and volunteers to develop portfolios by which their current capabilities can be demonstrated in the work context and be assessed for accreditation (i.e. the awarding of a full or part NVQ at level 1, 2, 3, 4 or 5). This provides formal recognition of their current skills and knowledge in the jobs that they do.

Particularly in the voluntary sector where often the level of qualifications are low, the possibility of gaining a nationally recognised qualification can be a tremendous motivating factor.

However, even without being used for individual accreditation purposes the relevant standards can be powerful tools in the recruitment and development of quality people in an organisation.

Sharpening the saw: developing staff

> Tell me and I will forget
> Show me and I may remember
> Involve me and I will understand

As Peter Drucker argues:

self-development is enmeshed with the mission of your organisation. Everyone involved with it, therefore, should ask, 'What, done really well, will make a difference to the organisation and me?' By concentrating on developing new skills, people take a bigger view of themselves and gain not just new capacities but self-respect. That translates into greater effectiveness on the job. (Drucker 1990)

As an aid to assessing training needs and drawing up training programmes the use of the national competency standards discussed above are tremendously valuable. However, there are several other factors which are important for an effective training and development process.

Achieving organisational goals

1. Training and development activities should reflect the specific aims, values, priorities and objectives contained in the strategic plan (see Chapter 2) and also the quality standards and procedures drawn up as part of any quality initiative (see Chapter 3). Training is only useful if it makes a contribution to achieving the aims and standards that the organisation has set. Too often individuals attend training courses which have no link to the needs of the organisation.

Evaluation

2. Linked to the above is the evaluation of training – not only

discovering whether, at the end of a particular training session, trainees feel it was enjoyable or interesting or not, but whether it enabled them to improve their effectiveness when back at their work. Did it help them to fulfil better the needs of the organisation as agreed in the strategic plan or achieve particular quality standards. This may involve an assessment by the individual some time after the training, and it might also involve an assessment by the individual's manager and even perhaps by colleagues and those the individual manages.

Investors in people

These two issues, ensuring that training is linked to organisational goals and the importance of evaluation, are key elements in the Investors in people award which is a nationally recognised framework for enabling an organisation to achieve its objectives and continuously improving its performance by investing in its people. It therefore provides an invaluable bench mark for an organisation in linking all of the discussions above on strategic planning and management, performance management, quality management and quality people. The award is based on four fundamental principles:

1. An investor in people makes a public commitment from the top to develop all employees to achieve its organisational objectives.
2. An investor in people regularly reviews the training and development needs of all employees.
3. An investor in people takes action to train and develop individuals on recruitment and throughout their employment.
4. An investor in people evaluates the investment in training and development to assess achievement and improve future effectiveness.

The award therefore looks for action under the following four headings:

- Commitment;
- Assessment of training needs;
- Action to train;
- Evaluation.

Commitment

The Investors in people award states:

a) Every organisation should have a written but flexible plan which sets out its goals and targets, considers how employees will contribute to achieving the plan and specifies how development needs in particular will be assessed and met;
b) Management should develop and communicate to all employees a vision of where the organisation is going and the contribution employees will make to its success, involving employee representatives as appropriate.

This is very consistent with the earlier section of this book on strategic planning and management, reinforcing the need to have a clear plan to involve as broad a group of staff as possible, to communicate this widely to all staff, and to show how the training and developments needs that arise from the plan will be assessed and met.

Assessment of training needs

The Investors in people award states:

a) The resources for training and developing employees should be clearly identified in the business plan;
b) Managers should be responsible for regularly agreeing training and development needs with each employee in the context of organisational objectives, setting targets and standards linked, where appropriate to the achievement of NVQs.

The issue of resources for training and development is an important one and should be linked into the strategic and operational planning process discussed earlier. It is vital if the objectives and standards that have been set are to be achieved that an appropriate budget needs to be agreed for the training and development of staff and volunteers.

Investors in people also says that managers should assess and agree what the training and development needs are of the people they manage in light of both the aims, principles, objectives and targets that arise from the strategic planning process *and* the national standards that are being developed for NVQs, discussed in the previous section. However, commitment and assessment are not enough. There needs to be action!

Action to train

The Investors in people award again requires evidence of two things:

a) action should focus on the training needs of all new recruits and continually develop and improve the skills of existing employees;
b) all employees should be encouraged to contribute to identifying and meeting their own job-related development needs.

This stresses a number of key points. All new staff and volunteers need a well thought out and planned induction. The improvement in the skills of existing trustees, staff and volunteers should not, however, be seen as a one-off activity but a continuous one. Lastly the role of the individual trustee, member of staff or volunteer in assessing and exploring ways of meeting their own training needs is crucial if it is to be successful. Learning cannot simply be imposed from above.

Evaluation

The Investors in people award stresses the importance of two key activities in relation to evaluation:

a) The investment, the competence and commitment of employees and the use made of skills learned, should be reviewed at all levels against organisational aims and targets;
b) The effectiveness of training and development should be reviewed at the top level and lead to renewed commitment and target setting.

This is an area that voluntary organisations are often weakest on. People are sent on a course or courses, or an internal course is organised, but the long-term value of such activities is rarely assessed. Investors in people looks not only for individual training and development activities to be evaluated against the specific objectives of the activities, but also that assessments are made at various levels in the organisation (including the top) of their contribution towards the organisational aims and objectives.

Investors in people is therefore an ideal framework to use in the voluntary sector for developing quality people who will be capable of achieving the organisation's objectives and quality standards which we discussed in previous chapters. It is intimately linked with the whole move towards a competence-based approach to recruitment, management and development represented by the development of clear and detailed standards as part of the NVQ initiative and discussed above.

Case study Potteries Housing Association

Potteries Housing Association (PHA) became committed to Investors in people in 1993 and was formally awarded the standard in October 1994, PHA provides emergency and move-on accommodation for homeless people. It opted for Investors in people for two main reasons: organisational profile and commitment to staff.

Staffordshire TEC provided funding for consultancy help in writing a business plan. NVQs already in place at PHA were seen as part of the Investors in people implementation process.

Danny Flynn, manager at one of PHA's projects, feels that although the process of gaining Investors in people was complicated, the benefits outweigh the initial work. Long-term, Investors in people means that PHA will still be providing services from a secure funding base, the services will be better and the staff will benefit. 'Quality marks are becoming necessary for voluntary organisation ... We've got to work within a market world to provide and be seen to provide a high quality service,' he says.

NCVO News Nov 1994

The experience of one voluntary organisation linking NVQs, Investors in people, and total quality management is given in the SHAW Homes case study.

Case study

From submission to measurable quality care: SHAW Homes

Introduction

Having successfully introduced NVQs into SHAW Homes, a national 'not for profit' organisation providing homes for those in need, I became increasingly aware of how NVQ competencies/standards could give structure to a Total Quality Management System by:

- Producing nursing/residential home standards based on NVQ standards.
- Instigating a 12-monthly care audit reflecting these standards and providing measurable system for monitoring care.
- Designing competency-based job descriptions based on a variety of NVQs – including care, management, catering, gardening, etc. These are job-specific and although not identical to the specific standards, give a measurable basis on which to assess individuals' performance.
- Planning competency based inductions which are based around core skills – care staff are expected to perform competently in these specified areas within 1–8 weeks of employment. This can be used as evidence when people register for NVQs in the future.
- Ensuring that all staff are expected to be assessed in their role-managers, care staff, etc., within a time limit of being in post. This helps to ensure everyone is working to a minimum specified standard (within the job description), and provides a way of monitoring performance and establishing training needs.

- Setting up a four-monthly appraisal system which ensures a formal review and monitoring of progress, and helps establish a departmental training needs analysis.
- Putting in place a training needs analysis process which established where the training gaps are and provision is made to fill these. This, along with 'in house training' which covers the majority of NVQ units, equal opportunities and value base days, provides the organisation with the basis of staff development.
- Training our own assessors and registering with CCETSW when they are approved. This will reduce costs dramatically and also help to ensure a standard assessment process.
- Ensuring that all assessors are either qualified nurses or team leaders. This decision was taken to ensure all assessors have a good knowledge base and have assessed previously. (We recognise previous assessments were not NVQs and address this issue in training.)
- Ensuring that individual and organisation business plans reflect human resource issues. To ensure the quality of care within the homes is of the highest standard, and the organisation's future is secure, regular monitoring and assessment of staff is essential.
- Working towards Investors in people for SHAW Homes which has given structure to the processes described.
- Making sure the business plan links back to the start of this flowchart which incorporates home standards and maintaining provision of a quality service.

Following this process I introduced some costings: assessor training – £225 per assessor; NVQ care level 2 – £1,308 per candidate. Most of these are unseen costs. It has provided a guideline when establishing provision of training. On the positive side, it can help to motivate staff when they realise the organisation is providing large amounts of money for their development.

We have developed a database taken from the CCETSW registration form information. This has given an easy way to provide CCETSW with 'facts and figures' when requested. Our candidates receive a certificate on completion of individual units for the NVQ, which was upon the request of the assessors.

Key tips

1. Get the managers 'on your side'. By mentioning NVQ or TQM a block or barrier is often established, possibly due to attitudes to training, cost or more work. By using standards and development it appears to encourage a less hostile reaction.
2. Show the links to the managers, and how it will benefit the service longer term by having a structure which is linked and is understood by all. This in itself is a motivator for individuals. When they see links and understand why they 'do what they do', it is the beginnings of a creative, loyal and enthusiastic staff member.

Dianne Gowdy

Key points

Crucial to the success of a voluntary organisation in achieving its 'vision of change' are the skills and knowledge of the trustees, staff and volunteers of the organisation.

The development of national standards, NVQs and 'Investors in people' provide a real opportunity to:

- Create much greater clarity about the competencies required to make individuals and teams more effective in achieving the organisation's aims and objectives.
- Recruit and select personnel in a more rational way.
- Identify training/development needs and identify ways of achieving them.
- Evaluate the impact of training/development activities and improve them.
- Provide accreditation for the skills and knowledge that the staff and volunteers have.

6 Quality managers

Chapter summary

Addressing the development needs of managers in voluntary organisations is crucial in ensuring that the sector can successfully take on the additional responsibilities that are being placed on it. This chapter looks at how national management standards developed by the management charter initiative (MCI) can be used to clarify the role of managers, recruit better managers, and provide them with appropriate development opportunities.

The whole range of changes that are highlighted in the introduction as having such a significant impact on the voluntary sector put a particular pressure on the energy and skills of managers who run voluntary organisations.

The kind of initiatives that are suggested in this book to make the voluntary sector more effective require an exceptionally high level of competence from these managers. They are very different in nature from the kinds of skills that would have been expected of them even five years ago, and probably very different from the kind of skills and aptitudes that brought them into the voluntary sector in the first place.

Ian Bruce has argued from his research of charity chief executives that the managerial:

attributes being looked for increasingly, are already scarce. This suggests the need for increased management development and training on the basis that it is insufficient at present, and will be needed even more in the future. This requirement is a challenge to all who are interested in the development of the voluntary sector and not-for-profit managers. (Bruce 1992)

He elsewhere argues that:

the charity sector is currently doing itself a disservice by failing to concentrate on management development, broadly defined. (Bruce 1992)

Fortunately, both the Investors in people framework and the competence-based approach discussed in Chapter 5 are as equally applicable to managers as they are to other staff or volunteers and integrate well into a strategic approach. The management charter initiative (MCI) has done some very useful work in clarifying the special skills required of a manager, which links in well to the concepts of strategic planning and management and quality management discussed above. The role of MCI and their code of practice is shown in Box 6.1 and is a useful framework for an organisation to establish a management development policy and strategy.

Box 6.1

The MCI aims and code

MCI's broad aims are:

- to increase employer awareness of management development issues;
  to promote the reform of management education and development;
- to develop and review the competence-based standards for all managers;
- to look at how the needs of experienced managers might be met;
- to develop other standards-based products that will contribute to improved management performance.

Each MCI employer signs a commitment to a 10-point code of good management development practice – a blueprint for improving managerial performance.

It is expected that management will communicate and demonstrate to all employees their commitment to the code. It is a formal recognition of the importance of management education and development.

> **Box 6.1** *continued*
>
> **MCI code**
>
> Organisations which are members of MCI commit themselves to:
>
> 1. Improve leadership and management skills;
> 2. Encourage continuous development;
> 3. Provide a coherent framework for self-development;
> 4. Ensure management development is integrated with work;
> 5. Provide access to training;
> 6. Encourage managers to gain relevant qualifications;
> 7. Participate in MCI networks;
> 8. Strengthen links with providers of management development;
> 9. Promote the challenge of management in local schools and colleges;
> 10. Review progress towards all these goals and set new targets.
>
> MCI Oct 1992

Although some of the terminology of the MCI management standards may initially be a little off-putting in the context of the voluntary sector, a little adaptation can easily make them feel very relevant to the role of a manager in a voluntary organisation.

In 1992, the NCVO commissioned Paddington Consultancy Partnership to look at the relevance of the national management standards for the voluntary sector and concluded that

> With a few Caveats, the MCI standards have provided a relevant, effective and comprehensive framework for exploring the development of organisational capacity in the voluntary sector (Baine *et al* 1994).

Work roles

The national management standards up to middle management

level are broken down into a number of 'key work roles' for managers:

- Managing people;
- Managing finance;
- Managing operations; and
- Managing information.

Units

As with other competency standards (see Chapter 5) these 'key work roles' are further broken down into 'units'. The full set of units for the current four key work roles for first line managers are given in Box 6.2.

The management standards are currently broken down into four main levels; one for supervisors (M1/S); one for first-line managers (M1); one for middle managers (M2); and one for senior managers. For accreditation purposes these standards form the respective competencies for NVQ level 3 (supervisory management); NVQ level 4 (first line management); and NVQ level 5 (middle management).

Box 6.2

M1 standards

The first line manager (M1) standards contain nine units as follows:

Key work roles		Units
Manage operations	1.1	Maintain and improve service and product operations.
	1.2	Contribute to the implementation of change in services, products and systems.
Manage finance	1.3	Recommend, monitor and control the use of resources.

> **Box 6.2** *continued*
>
> | Key work roles | | Units |
> |---|---|---|
> | Manage people | 1.4 | Contribute to the recruitment and selection of personnel. |
> | | 1.5 | Develop teams, individuals and self to enhance performance. |
> | | 1.6 | Plan, allocate and evaluate work carried out by teams, individuals and self. |
> | | 1.7 | Create, maintain and enhance effective working relationships. |
> | Manage information | 1.8 | Seek, evaluate and organise information for action. |
> | | 1.9 | Exchange information to solve problems and make decisions. |
>
> © Crown Copyright

In the M2 standards for middle managers, five of the nine units for first-line managers are also part of the middle management standards, primarily those concerned with managing people and information. This reinforces the view that there is a core set of skills and attributes that all managers need to have. These are then built on to create a broader and more complex set of standards for middle managers (M2) (Box 6.3).

> **Box 6.3**
>
> **M2 standards**
>
> The units for middle-manager (M2) standards are as follows:
>
> Manage operations
> 1. Initiate and implement change and improvements in services, products and systems.

Box 6.3 *continued*

2. Monitor, maintain and improve service and product delivery.

Manage finance

3. Monitor and control the use of resources.
4. Secure effective resource allocation for activities and projects.

Manage people

5. Recruit and select personnel.
6. Develop teams, individuals and self to enhance performance.
7. Plan, allocate and evaluate work carried out by teams, individuals and self.
8. Create, maintain and enhance effective working relationships.

Manage information

9. Seek, evaluate and organise information for action.
10. Exchange information to some problems and make decisions.

© Crown Copyright

Box 6.4

Elements

As with other competency standards, the units are further broken down into various elements. For example the M2 units and elements for the key work role of 'managing people' are as follows:

Box 6.4 *continued*

Units	Elements
5. Recruit and select personnel	5.1 Define future personnel requirements.
	5.2 Determine specifications to secure quality people.
	5.3 Assess and select candidates against team and organisation requirements.
6. Develop teams, individuals and self to enhance performance	6.1 Develop and improve teams through planning activities.
	6.2 Identify, review and improve development activities for individuals.
	6.3 Develop oneself within the job role.
	6.4 Evaluate and improve the development processes used.
7. Plan, allocate and evaluate work carried out by teams, individuals and self	7.1 Set and update work objectives for teams and individuals.
	7.2 Plan activities and determine work methods to achieve objectives.
	7.3 Allocate work and evaluate teams, individuals and self against objectives.
	7.4 Provide feedback to teams and individuals on their performance.
8. Create, maintain and enhance effective working relationships	8.1 Establish and maintain the trust and support of one's subordinates.

> **Box 6.4** *continued*
>
> | Units | Elements |
> |---|---|
> | | 8.2 Establish and maintain the trust and support of one's immediate manager. |
> | | 8.3 Establish and maintain relationships with colleagues. |
> | | 8.4 Identify and minimise interpersonal conflict. |
> | | 8.5 Implement disciplinary and grievance procedures. |
> | | 8.6 Counsel staff. |
>
> © Crown Copyright

The complete set of units and elements for M1 and M2 are included in Appendix 2. Even at this level of detail you soon realise the complexity and depth involved in the job of being a manager even before you consider any of the specialist, functional or occupational aspects (e.g. care, housing, administration, etc.) that are also inevitably part of a manager's job.

> **Box 6.5**
>
> **Performance criteria**
>
> As with other competency standards each element is further broken down into 'performance criteria'. So for example the element 'define future personnel requirements' which is part of the 'recruit and select personnel' unit has the following 'performance criteria'.
>
> a) The required competencies and attributes of individuals and teams, and the inter-relationships between the two, are clearly identified.

> **Box 6.5** *continued*
>
> b) Organisational objectives and constraints which will affect staff levels are clearly identified.
> c) The views of appropriate members of staff are adequately taken into account.
> d) Estimates of personnel needs are supported by appropriate calculations, where necessary.
> e) Information used is correct, valid and reliable.
> f) Information is presented on time, is accurate to the level required and contains the necessary amount of detail.
>
> © Crown Copyright

The management standards describe expected outputs and outcomes, i.e. what a manager should be able to do competently. Being results-focused has many advantages and makes it much more likely that the individual manager will achieve the performance and targets that the organisation requires. Some other management competency frameworks (not NVQ) focus much more on the underlying skills, knowledge and attitudes required in a job. Some of these frameworks have been drawn from detailed research into the underlying characteristics of a good manager, often asking the views of managers themselves what they consider to be the attributes of 'a good manager'.

Personal effectiveness model

To complement its work in developing the M1 and M2 management standards, (which are output and outcome orientated), MCI have developed their own input model of 'personal effectiveness' highlighting the key underlying qualities that a competent manager needs to develop. These are very useful in clarifying some of the 'personal characteristics' of a person specification used in recruitment and also in appraising individual managers. The MCI personal effectiveness model is given in Appendix 3, and provides detailed behaviours associated with each dimension.

Senior managers

MCI have also more recently agreed a set of national standards for senior managers, which are both very relevant to senior managers in the voluntary sector and closely linked to the concepts of strategic planning and management discussed earlier. These senior management standards give the key purpose as 'To develop and implement strategies to further the organisation's mission'. The standards are then grouped under four key areas of action:

- understanding and influencing the environment;
- setting the strategy and gaining commitment;
- planning, implementing and monitoring;
- evaluating and improving performance.

Figure 6.1 gives an indication of the iterative nature of the strategic planning and implementation process.

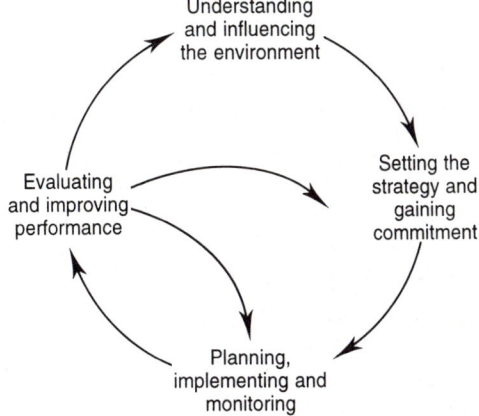

Figure 6.1 MCI senior management model.

Half of these key areas are broken down into the following more detailed units.

Understanding and influencing the environment:

- External trends;

- Internal strengths and weaknesses;
- Stakeholders.

Setting the strategy and gaining commitment:

- Setting the strategy and gaining commitment.

Planing, implementing and monitoring:

- Programmes, projects and plans;
- Delegation and action;
- Culture;
- Monitoring.

Evaluating and improving performance:

- Evaluating and improving performance.

Like the other management standards these are further broken down into elements, performance criteria and range statements.

It can be seen even from this limited level of detail that these senior management standards are closely related to the model outlined earlier in relation to strategic planning and management, and would form a very useful alternative checklist for senior managers in the voluntary sector in developing their strategic management capability.

As with the other levels of management standards, the senior management standards also have a list of key underlying skills or personal competencies which are needed to enable a senior manager to be effective. These are:

- Judgement;
- Self-confidence;
- Strategic perspective;
- Achievement focus;
- Communication;
- Information search;
- Building teams;
- Influencing others.

The standards themselves give the 'key behaviours' which should be evident from each of these eight personal competencies.

Uses of the management standards

Having involved the appropriate managers in the process of customising ('contextualising' in the jargon) the national management standards for the organisation a very powerful tool will have been created which will help the organisation do a number of things:

- Clarify the roles of managers and enable the organisation improve their job descriptions;
- Draw up or review the person specifications of managerial posts which indicate the qualities that the organisation is looking for in candidates when recruiting;
- Appraise and review the performance of managers against clear objective criteria (i.e. the appropriate standards for the post and the personal competencies);
- Assess the training needs of managers against clear objective criteria (i.e. the appropriate standards for the post);
- Develop a management development strategy and programmes which will both meet the development needs of the individual manager in his/her job and the needs of the organisation to achieve its objectives and standards, and to continuously improve;
- Develop a framework for evaluating management development activities (internal and external).

In addition to these six very common uses the management standards framework can also be used to:

- Develop a job evaluation framework against which posts (not individuals) can be evaluated and allocated to a particular salary grade;
- Develop a 'succession strategy' to enable individuals to develop the necessary skills to be able to eventually undertake a more senior post.

And, of course, there are also a range of advantages for the individual manager who should be much clearer about what is expected of him or her in his or her job: how he or she is getting on; what his or her training needs are and how they might be met. In addition because the MCI national management standards are the competency standards for NVQs in management, the individual manager has the possibility of developing a portfolio of evidence which can be assessed for the awarding of a full or partial (any number of units) NVQ in management (level 4 or 5).

Evaluation

Like all training and development activities, the evaluation of the activity is crucial not only to demonstrate the impact on the individual, which may be assessed by the individual or his or her manager at the end of the activity or some time later, but also on the organisation in relation to organisational objectives. Figure 6.2 gives a very useful model, developed in the public sector, but equally applicable to the voluntary sector.

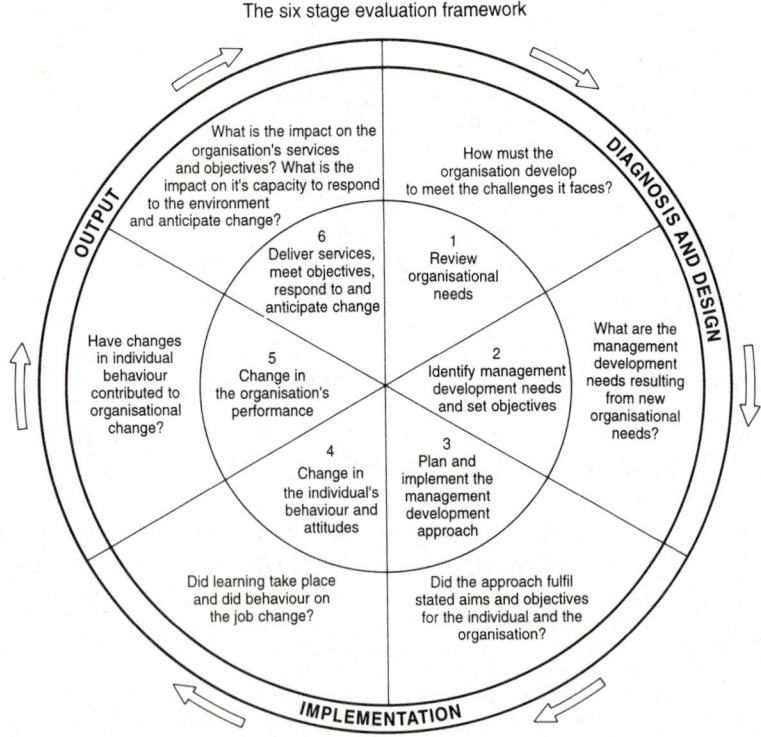

Figure 6.2 Stages in the development of the organisation and evaluation of management developments.

Experience in a wide variety of organisations would indicate that to be successful, management development must:

- Be central to organisational change.
- Be inseparable from organisational development.
- Be related to and designed to support organisational strategy.
- Be owned and managed by the organisation and its managers.
- Have the active support of senior managers and the management/executive committee.
- Use a variety of methods and techniques and not be reliant on off-the-job external courses (see Box 6.6).
- Be related to the needs of individuals in their job roles.
- Be seen to achieve results and be systematically evaluated.
- Focus on the development of competencies required of an excellent manager.
- Be adequately budgeted for.
- Be seen as a long-term investment in the future of the organisation.

When people think about training they usually think about external or internal formally presented courses. These are often far from satisfactory in meeting the real needs of the participants. In fact most learning probably takes place in a very different way, where doing and learning can come together.

To maximise learning the whole range of learning opportunities and methods need to be considered (see Box 6.6).

Box 6.6

Some methods of meeting management development needs

- Observation;
- Coaching;
- Mentoring;
- Job enlargement;
- Job enrichment;
- Reading;
- Video;

> **Box 6.6** *continued*
>
> - Audio cassettes;
> - Computer-aided learning;
> - Action learning sets;
> - Special projects;
> - Secondment;
> - Placement;
> - Workshops;
> - Games and simulations;
> - Short courses;
> - Evening classes;
> - Open/distance learning;
> - Long courses (part-time and full-time).

Key points

- There is an urgent need for increased management training and development in the voluntary sector.
- MCI national management standards provide an appropriate framework to
  - help clarify the roles of managers in voluntary organisations
  - help recruit better managers
  - help assess and meet managers' training/development needs
  - appraise managers performance.
- Senior management standards provide an alternative framework for strategic planning and organisational development.
- The evaluation of all training and development activities is vitally important.
- There are a range of ways of meeting management development needs, not just formal courses.

7 Putting it all together

Chapter summary

This final chapter pulls together the key themes outlined throughout the book, and endeavours to integrate all the initiatives presented into an overall model, highlight some general key themes and look at how a voluntary organisation might start the process of introducing these initiatives.

Initiatives

The previous chapters provide a brief tour of a range of models, techniques, initiatives and benchmarks that have tremendous potential in the voluntary sector: They include:

- Strategic planning and management;
- Performance management;
- Quality Assurance and management;
- Competence-based management;
- National Vocational Qualifications;
- Investors in people;
- Management standards and development.

Although it is possible to see them simply as separate but overlapping individual initiatives (indeed the momentum for each comes from a different source and often the terminology used is different), I believe that they are much more powerful if looked at together. It doesn't mean doing them all at once, which can cause a feeling of 'initiative overload', but it does mean developing an integrated vision of the future management of the organisation and then planning a programme (perhaps over three or five years) to work toward this vision a bit at a time. It is important to 'think total, but build Piecemeal'.

Key themes

A number of important inter-related themes run through all these initiatives and have kept recurring throughout this book:

- Clarifying and meeting the needs and expectations of the beneficiaries;
- Clarifying and achieving organisational goals;
- Creating clarity and unity of purpose at all levels;
- Establishing and consistently achieving clear standards;
- Ensuring continuous review, evaluation and improvement;
- Clarifying and meeting the development needs of staff, volunteers, managers and trustees;
- Empowering individuals to develop and achieve the goals of the organisation by creating the appropriate culture.

Based on these themes all the initiatives outlined in earlier chapters can be integrated within one comprehensive model, as is shown in Figure 7.1. This probably looks a little daunting, and raises the obvious question of where does an organisation start?

Each of the elements of the model are designed to be continuously developing, that is they involve a continuous cycle of planning, action, review and planning again, and so on (Figure 7.2). The process of organisational development over a period might more simply be represented as shown in Figure 7.3. This recognises that as well as periods of great progress there are likely to be periods where the organisation doesn't feel as if it is moving forward at all, particularly during the review and planning phases of the individual cycles. There is no doubt that the initiatives presented in this book take a very significant amount of time and effort to work through and to show results. There are even likely to be periods where the staff and volunteers involved feel that the concentration on planning and implementing a new initiative is in fact having a detrimental effect on their work (the downward parts of the cycle) because of the time and effort involved in making any significant new initiative happen. It takes a period of time to elapse for the benefits to be seen in practice,

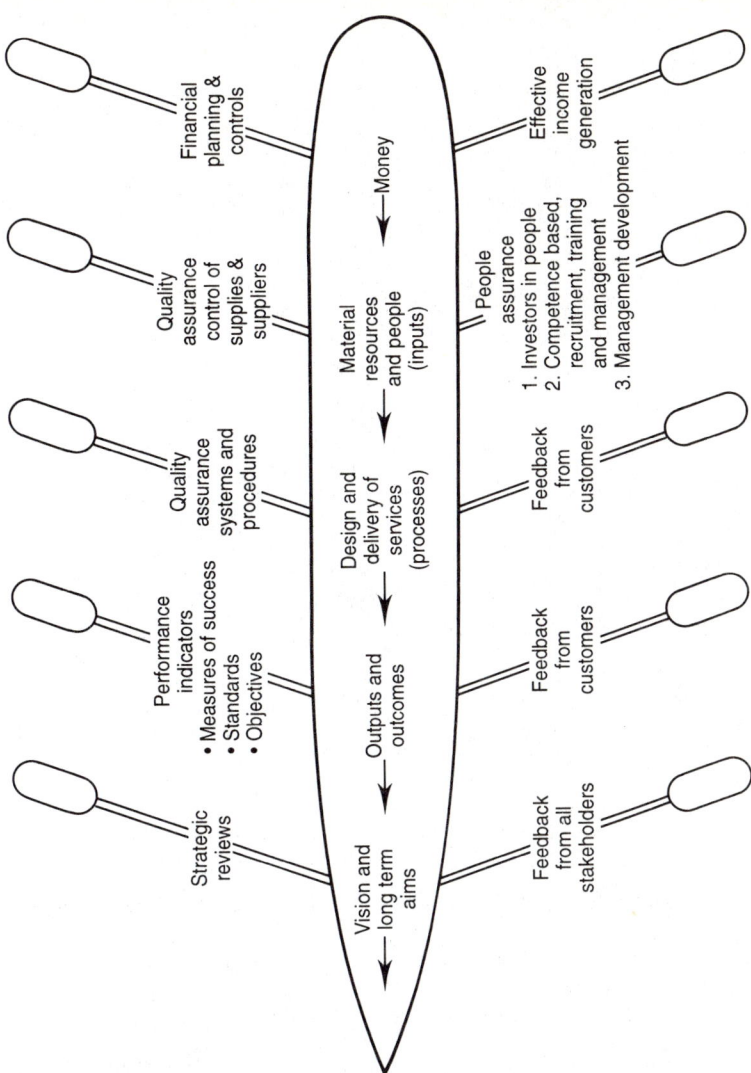

Figure 7.1 The quest for excellence. An organisational development model.

rather than just in theory. Also, once the initial hurdle of putting in place new systems, etc. is got over then there is considerably less work and anxiety involved in the next phase. It is important, however, not to underestimate the human implications of change.

138 Putting it all together

Figure 7.2 Plan/act/review cycle.

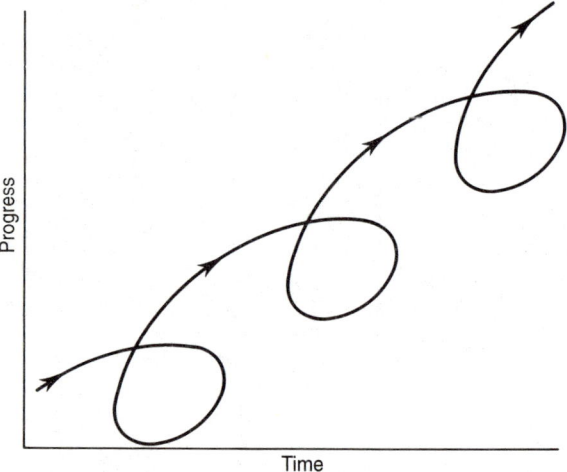

Figure 7.3 Organisational development over a period of time.

Where to start?

As mentioned earlier, many organisations start the process of pro-active organisational development with an evaluation/review which is usually imposed on them by a statutory funder. Often this evaluation highlights the need for work on strategic planning, quality, staff development etc.

Some organisations may have their own powerful reasons to start with one of the particular initiatives highlighted in this book. For example, there may be a very clear need to establish a system for giving staff and volunteers regular feedback on their performance and establish personal development plans to improve their skills. In that case the Investors in people framework would be a particularly appropriate place to start, forcing the organisation to look not only at these things but also at the strategic plans that should guide the priorities for the feedback and development.

Alternatively, if there is a strong need to enable staff and volunteers to achieve some form of recognised qualification, and the organisation wants to improve the recruitment and development of staff, the creation of a competence-based approach using NVQ standards as outlined in Chapter 5 would be a good starting point, and links in very well with the Investors in people approach.

Perhaps the organisation has expanded rapidly and promoted a number of individuals relatively new to management. The national management standards provide an excellent starting point in helping to clarify their roles and enabling them to develop their skills as managers. The senior management standards also provide their own strategic planning model for an organisation to use as a checklist of good practice in strategic planning and management.

The key problem that an organisation faces may be uncertainty as to whether it is consistently meeting the needs of the beneficiaries of the organisation's services; or services are not improving in the way that was hoped; or staff or volunteers don't see maintaining and developing the quality of the services as anything to do with them; or different parts of the organisation don't work well together – poor communication resulting in unnecessary mistakes; or suppliers not delivering the appropriate goods or services at the right time. Any of these problems would indicate that perhaps the initial focus should be on quality assurance and management.

There may be a problem with the actual performance of individuals in relation to the overall plans of the organisation. The individuals may not be clear about what is expected of them and what their contribution to the overall vision and aims of the organisation actually is; or they may not receive any feedback on how they are doing and whether it is what is expected; or they may not currently have the right level of skills and knowledge. In these circumstances a strong focus on performance management might be the most effective tool, perhaps again using the Investors in people framework.

In one sense it doesn't matter at all what part of the model an organisation begins with as each of the tools and models are of value in themselves. However, there is considerable logic in starting with the strategic planning process outlined at the beginning of the book. This creates an ultimate vision of where the organisation wants to go, and should include commitments to meeting the needs of the beneficiaries, continuous improvement and the development of staff, etc. All the detailed aspects of development and training etc. should all flow from this ultimate vision and should be building blocks in achieving the goals of the organisation.

To conclude, here are some key points about introducing change as part of the process of enabling an organisation to develop.

Key points

- Don't try to introduce all the initiatives at once – begin with the most important one first and build on it.
- Consult and involve everyone – build a wide sense of ownership of any change.
- Think total, but build piecemeal.
- Seek regular feedback from beneficiaries and act on it.
- Ensure active commitment from the top (staff and committee).
- Ensure communication is open, clear and jargon-free.
- Ensure that all departmental and unit policies, strategies and programmes are closely linked to the overall strategy of the organisation.
- Ensure that individual and team achievements are praised, and organisational achievements are celebrated!
- Don't re-invent the wheel – learn from the experiences and expertise of others who have been down the same path before.
- Keep at it – perseverance will pay off.

8 Two case studies

Major case study 1

In the early 1980's homelessness had been increasing rapidly and putting the very limited resources of the Belfast Simon community under pressure. The community was also receiving a considerable number of referrals from outside of Belfast where little temporary accommodation existed. The basic Simon principles established by the Founder in the early 1960's were perceived as significantly outdated (no paid staff or government funding).

In response to these pressures the staff, committee and volunteers undertook a strategic review which resulted in a fundamental redefining of the overall purpose, aims and principles of the organisation. It was also agreed to change the name to Simon Community Northern Ireland to reflect the planned development of projects outside of Belfast.

Three years later the development of new projects was slower than had been hoped for because of the difficulty in obtaining funds particularly from private sources. A further although briefer strategic review produced a very concise draft strategic statement (2 pages) of what the Simon Community was, what it had achieved to date, why its work was not only needed but also needed to be significantly expanded. A third page listed the new projects that could be developed if £0.5M could be raised from the private sources (unlocking significant public funds).

This three page draft photocopy was used on dozens of occasions in the following three years (and went through many drafts) to engage potential funders in a discussion of the urgent needs and what their financial support could achieve. The potential funders were always approached on the basis of their 'advice and guidance' being sought on the draft ideas contained in the brief strategy document. The draft document, in fact, never became a finally approved document and was never produced as a glossy brochure, but levered almost £1M of private funds and enabled ten new accommodation projects to open which wouldn't have otherwise got off the ground.

Significant growth of the organisation also highlighted a number of other difficulties which included:

1. The staff (including managers) and volunteers attracted to the organisation tended to be unqualified and often of limited educational attainment, although with significant skills and experience.
2. It became more difficult to be sure that the standards that were expected in all the residential projects were being carried out consistently.

A comprehensive strategic review carried out in 1993 created a formal mission statement for the first time as follows:

Simon is the principal cross community voluntary organisation working and campaigning for the elimination of homelessness throughout Northern Ireland. We are committed to achieving this by providing accommodation, support and resettlement services for individuals who are homeless or threatened with homelessness which assist them to achieve their full potential and rights as citizens.

This was further broken down into five specific long-term aims as follows:

Aims

1. That all individuals who are homeless have access to:
   - a range of temporary accommodation options
   - resilient and support services that offer assistance in obtaining and successfully remaining in appropriate long-term accommodation.

2. That all individuals who are threatened with homelessness have access to the information, support and advice they need in order to prevent them from becoming homeless.
3. That the politics and practices of government and relevant bodies both help to prevent homelessness and meet the needs and aspirations of people who become homeless.
4. That the potential of human, financial and material resources available to the organisation is maximised.
5. That sufficient income is generated to enable the organisation to achieve its goals.

(Simon Community Northern Ireland 1994)

A set of revised principles was agreed which emphasised the values and culture of the organisation, as follows:

Simon Community Strategic Plan 1994–1999
PRINCIPLES

Simon is fully committed to the following principles which form the basis of the culture of the Simon Community and should be manifest throughout the organisation.

Effectiveness
Giving paramount importance to the needs and aspirations of individuals who are homeless. Continually improving quality standards which meet the needs of individuals who are homeless, referral agencies, funders, staff and volunteers and which comply with legal obligations. Providing a diversity of services that offer choice and are flexible in meeting the different needs of individuals.

Equity
Ensuring that everyone is treated with dignity and respect and that each individual's identity, beliefs and choices are acknowledged and respected.

Independence and choice
Encouraging and supporting individuals who are homeless to attain their optimum level of independence, to exercise

informed personal choice and to maximise their potential and their rights as citizens.

Participation
Actively promoting the involvement of individuals in decisions that may affect them.

Competent and valued staff and volunteers
Providing a coherent framework for continuous self-development, which is integrated with the work, creates access to training and provides the opportunity to gain relevant accredited qualifications where possible.

Efficiency
Making efficient use of all the physical and human resources of the organisation.

Health and safety
Actively promoting the health and safety of residents, staff, volunteers and visitors and ensuring compliance with all relevant legal requirements.

Co-operation
Working in close co-operation with other relevant agencies to meet the needs of individuals who are homeless.

Redress
Actively seeking and responding to the views of people who are homeless, funders, referral agencies, staff and volunteers.

Ensuring that there are clear effective and swift procedures for internal and external complaints or grievances and that these are appropriately investigated to prevent any recurrence of similar problems in future.

NB: These principles are not given in any particular order of priority.

An annual operational planning process was established with very specific and assessable objectives, under each aim, for each year.

The objectives for the first year, as well as focusing on a whole range of proposals for increasing the amount of accommodation and other services to people who are homeless, including the following:

- Putting in place a quality assurance system – BS5750 (now BS EN ISO 9000) within the context of a continuous improvement (TQM) programme.
- Start the process of making NVQs available to all staff and volunteers.

Year 2 operational plan (1995/6) included:

- Assessment of the quality assurance system.
- Further work to keep up the momentum of the continuous improvement programme.
- Expansion of the NVQ programmes within the organisation.
- Improving the evaluation of training within the organisation.
- Commitment to assessment under the Investors in people award.
- The customising of MCI national management standards for use in the recruitment and development of managers.

Issues

The key problem that arose in carrying out this ambitious programme was the pressure that many first-line and middle managers have felt under in implementing a number of new initiatives at the same time.

In hindsight it may well have been easier and more successful to agree a more staged programme, perhaps commencing with the Investors in people framework and NVQs.

In each of the initiatives undertaken, the organisation probably underestimated the amount of time, commitment and training it would require, even with outside support, to gain a sense of ownership from all the staff and to get the new systems firmly embedded.

There was also a tendency for the operational parts of the organisation, e.g. those managing in the residential units, to perceive each new initiative as something of an imposition on an already pressurised workload and a distraction from their real work. This reinforces the need to spend more time in generating a feeling of ownership of the strategic and operational planning processes and being realistic about what can be achieved in a short timescale.

Having said all that, clearly very substantial progress has been made in achieving the aims and principles of the organisation, greatly aided by the various models, frameworks and ideas which have been outlined in the preceding chapters.

Major case study 2

Sense

In 1995 Sense set out its mission and agreed a strategic plan to take it up to the new millenium. The mission clarifies Sense's fundamental purpose and core beliefs. It re-states Sense's priority to work with and for people who are deafblind and has been prepared through a process of consultation and involvement of trustees, staff and users of Sense services.

Each region and department also has a plan. Sense uses the strategic plan to guide their preparation of the operational plans and budgets that determine what we do each year. This planning process is very important as Sense continues to grow and becomes more complex and we find ourself working in a rapidly changing environment.

The preparation of the plan involved people across the organisation. The process has distinct stages:

1. A steering group of staff, committee members and a family forum member met over a period of 15 months and oversaw the planning and consultation process.
2. All regions and departments reviewed the achievements of the last four years and any lessons to be learnt.
3. Brainstorming meetings were held and groups met to consider residential services, training, education and quality issues.

4. Initial plans were produced for all Sense activities.
5. A weekend meeting of the committee and senior staff considered the plans and issues. Recommendations were made for incorporation in the final plans.
6. People who use Sense services were consulted with branches and family forum commenting and a day event being held for users. Comments were fed back into the planning process from these and other meetings and events.
7. The final plans were produced and agreed by Council.

This plan is Sense's fourth. The last plan anticipated substantial growth and many aspirations were fulfilled and often developments surpassed projections. They have continued to develop high quality services and to raise the profile of the needs of sensory-impaired people with the aim of creating real change in individuals' lives and in the community.

The proposals contained in this plan build on Sense's recent growth. 1995 will see Sense's expenditure exceed £19 million.

There are a number of substantial developments planned for 1995–9 throughout the United Kingdom which will require large outlays of funding. Finance will also be needed for the development of a wide range of outreach services to support deafblind people in community housing, at home or in other residential settings.

Mission statement

Sense is a national voluntary organisation that works and campaigns with and for people who have a sensory disability. Our priority is people who are deafblind – which means a severe impairment of both vision and hearing resulting in unique and special needs. In addition we work with people with a single sensory impairment and other disabilities. We provide advice, support, information and services for individual people, their families, carers and involved professionals.

Sense's values

Sense believes that everyone:

- has rights and responsibilities and is entitled to dignity and respect;
- has the right to quality services to meet individual needs;
- has the right to opportunities which will promote individual development;
- has the right to information;
- has the right to make choices;
- should be able to contribute to the development of services directly or through a representative, family member or advocate.

Sense's aims

These are to:

- provide a range of quality services across the UK including family support, children's services, residential and community services, continuing education and advocacy;
- work to develop new projects and services, either as an organisation or in partnership with others;
- campaign for greater public, political and legal recognition of needs and action to meet needs;
- manage our operations – including fund-raising and finances – in the most effective manner.

Sense's strategic plan summary

The priority user group for Sense is clarified as people who are deafblind. In addition we work with people with a single sensory impairment and other disabilities. Of course all service users will be equally valued irrespective of the nature of their disability.

Within the deafblind population Sense will continue to

emphasise work with congenitally deafblind people and with children and young adults. In addition to residential services and continuing education we will now prioritise other community services, family support, children's services, and advocacy. While continuing to work with people with Usher syndrome we will provide services for other people with acquired deafblindness. This will be mainly funded through contracts but will also involve some fund-raising. Work with older deafblind people with sensory loss acquired very late in life will develop mainly through partnerships, training and campaigning work rather that direct service delivery.

Campaigning remains a priority.

Sense will continue to focus on development through undertaking a programme of direct provision and by encouraging other providers.

The priority for regional development in the past has been residential homes for people with congenital deafblindness or multiple disability. While continuing to develop and establish new homes in areas without services, this will no longer be given a higher priority than other community services. Day services will be opened up to non-residential users and will be developed as separate services. This diversification is in line with the development of community care practice and the provision of a range of options giving choice to families and users. Such services will include assessment, outreach, day services, respite, intervenor/enabler schemes and communicator-guide schemes.

Sense now has some services established or under development in most regions of the UK. There are staff with development responsibility in the West, East, South East, Wales, Northern Ireland and Scotland. A new priority for development is the North of England.

There will be seven divisions within the UK: Sense Scotland (a wholly-owned subsidiary charity), Sense Cymru, Sense Northern Ireland and four English regions; Sense West, Sense East, Sense South East and eventually Sense North.

Many of Sense's services have national catchment

areas and many users live far away from the family home. Residential services will move towards having regional catchment areas. There will be no imposed movement of people as choice for the user and the user's family is most important. Some services may be designated as specialist and national because of low incidence and need for specialisms.

A vital part of Sense's service provision is our front line response to people with disabilities, families and carers, and professionals. This is the role of the Regional Advisory Service and this is a priority for expansion in order to provide a national service with consistent standards. At least one post is to be funded from fund-raised income in each major geographical region. Other posts will be established with funding from local authorities but a service will be available to all through charitable income.

Family (Education) Advisory Service staff cover some parts of England and provide a service with an emphasis on families with young children. There are no opportunities for such support in many parts of the UK. In recent years the Family (Education) Advisory Service has had to cover all costs from fees and grants. The importance of early intervention is recognised and as a result a minimum level of education support of one day each week in each region is to be found from fund-raised income. Other support will continue to be provided where contracts and grants allow this to happen.

The values adopted by Sense in the revised Mission Statement relate to service users, volunteers and staff, and will guide management practice and service provision.

Quality standards will be established for all Sense activities and evaluation and monitoring will take place regularly.

Priority for spending money from charitable appeals is innovative projects, seed funds for new services and specifically agreed charitable objectives. Functions that provide support to direct services will increasingly be funded through the general services charge – this is a charge levied on all Sense activity. Staff training will be improved by setting up a special National Staff Development Section.

As well as providing services, the Policy and National Services Department at head office will lead on promotional work (e.g. Education team); policy development; development of service models and support to services (e.g. Guide–Help/Communicator–Guide Development Project, Usher service, Adviser on congenital deafblindness, Education team). Some work will take place on equal access to services. Branches and user involvement are recognised as important. The national services include holidays; assessment and outreach training; casework and advocacy. They include innovative and developmental projects.

A review of education provision for deafblind children, likely future provision, and Sense's possible roles will be undertaken. A clear policy will be developed on rights to education. As in other service areas, Sense will plan and seek to develop research, monitoring and quality assurance related to education. A proposal to the Department for Education for research on education practice including that developed through GEST (Grants for Education Support and Training: multi-sensory impairment funding ends March 1995) will be funded.

Sense will further develop systems for recording need and using such information. In particular a priority is to identify school leavers and people in the family home cared for by elderly parents – in order to be able to promote the development of services to meet their needs.

Sense international work will be integrated with other activities. A major service will be developed during the period. Financing of international work will be from new sources.

Finally, Sense reiterates the importance of users, families and professionals as partners.

Lessons learnt

1. How you go about strategic planning depends on

where you are in your development stage. (Sense's current strategic planning process was a monumental affair lasting a year.)
2. To have a clear sense of an organisation's direction over forthcoming years has been tremendously useful.
3. It has been very valuable to have a reference point when considering unplanned opportunities that have arisen.
4. The most important thing is to involve all stakeholders. The process is a marvellous way of uniting people, if sensitively handled.

Appendix 1: UK Quality Award – Learning from the success of others

The self assessment framework and measurement processes described in *The British Quality Foundation UK Quality award Self Assessment Guide* provide the basis to measure corporate excellence. They intentionally **do not**, provide a 'prescription' on what to do to improve an organisation's performance.

Similarly, it is not the intention of this book to provide such guidance, which must, of course, be organisation specific and prioritised against what would be of maximum use to the organisation and the achievement of its strategic plans. However, it can be useful to understand what excellent organisations, who are scoring highly against these measures, are typically doing.

Experiences gained from organisations world-wide have shown that certain aims, values, activities or practices are often common in organisations that have either won awards or scored highly in self assessments. The lists below show possible 'excellence indicators' for each of the nine assessment criteria. These indicators are tabled to aid learning and to prompt thoughts on what aims, values, activities or practices may be worthy of further evaluation in your own organisation.

Key excellence indicators

1. *Key excellence indicators for leadership*
   - Strong commitment to employee satisfaction from leaders;
   - Strong customer and supplier focus from leaders;
   - Managers develop 'role model' behaviours;
   - Highly visible ('missionary') leaders;

- Clear, easily remembered values;
- Managers acting as coaches;
- Managers act as champions for corporate citizenship and impact on society;
- Managers give and receive training.

2. *Key excellence indicators for policy and strategy*

- Vision and values reflect principles of total quality and customer satisfaction;
- Aggressive ('leapfrog') goals;
- Strong cycle time drivers;
- 'Quality' planning integrated with business planning;
- Long term horizons in planning;
- Aggressive planning 'drivers' (benchmarks) derived from study of world leaders;
- Key targets derived from customer requirements and deployed to all units;
- Plans driven from and linked to suppliers and customers;
- Policy and strategy developed from feedback from customers, suppliers and people within organisations.

3. *Key excellence indicators for people management*

- Human resource plans integrated with strategic plans;
- 'Internal customer' concepts used;
- Comprehensive training and education programmes with relevance/effectiveness continuously reviewed;
- Empowerment, flexible assignments, people involvement encouraged;
- Team and individual recognition;
- Lower staff turnover, accidents, absenteeism.

4. *Key excellence indicators for resources*

- Internal customer concepts used;
- Focused to support key processes and policy and strategy;
- Regular reviews of effectiveness;
- Operationally integrated management systems.

5. *Key excellence indicators for processes*

- Clear definition of critical processes;

- Quantitative orientation – focus on actionable data;
- Widely deployed, accessible data;
- Multiple measures;
- Interlinking measures – external and internal;
- Challenging targets identified and used;
- Focus on response times;
- Quality systems standards (e.g. BS EN ISO 9000) in place;
- Integration of prevention and correction with daily operations;
- Linkage to suppliers.

6. *Key excellence indicators for customer satisfaction*

- Proactive customer systems leading to measures that customers perceive as relevant;
- Use of all 'listening posts':
    surveys;
    product/service follow-ups;
    complaints;
    turnover of customers;
    employees.
- Assessment of all relevant market segments;
- Surveys go beyond current customers;
- Results benchmarked against leaders.

7. *Key excellence indicators for people satisfaction*

- Perception measured and surveys that have proven relevance to employees;
- Results benchmarked to leaders;
- Inter and intra-organisation comparisons;
- Use of predictor, leading and influencing measures as well as direct perception surveys.

8 *Key excellence indicators for impact on society*

- Use of measures that directly indicate society's perception of the organisation;
- Results benchmarked against leaders;
- Significant community support/partnerships;
- Exemplary practices with respect to preservation of global resources.

9 *Key excellence indicators for business results*
- Broad base of improvement trends in products, services, internal operations, cycle time, productivity, key processes, financial results;
- Results 'benchmarked' to leaders;
- Improvements in supplier quality.

Appendix 2: Management standards

M1 (first line management)

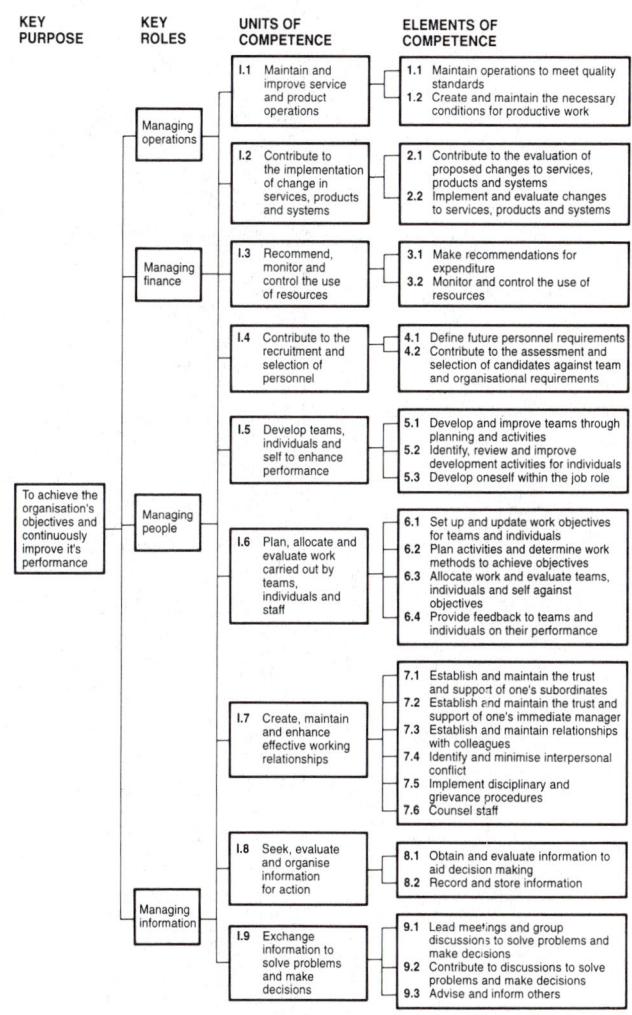

158   Appendix

M2 (middle management)

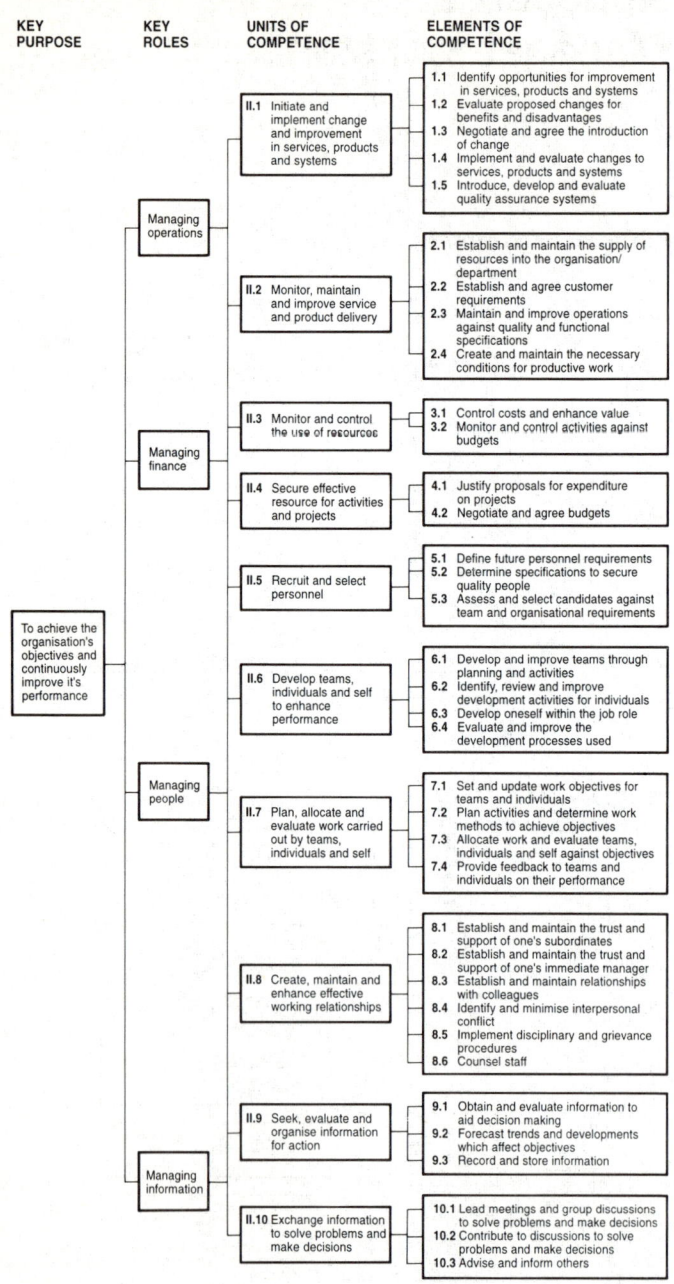

Appendix 3: Personal competence model

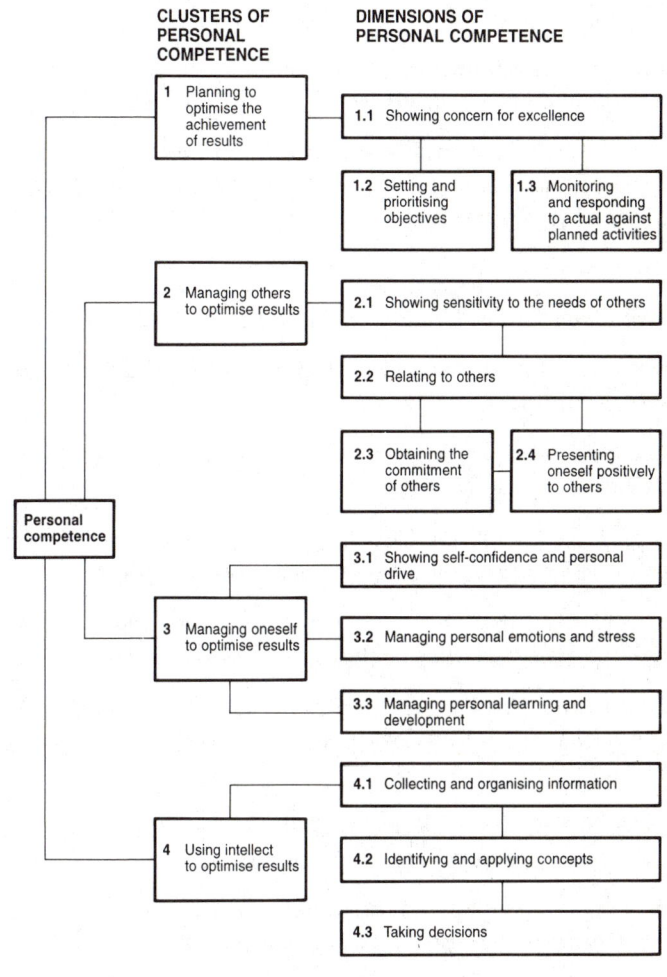

References

Armstrong, M. (1994) *Performance Management*, Kogan Page, London.

Baine, S., Coleman, N. and Hilditch, S. (1994) *Management Standards and the Voluntary Sector*, NCVO, London.

Batsleer, J., Cornforth, C. and Paton, R. (1991) *Issues in Voluntary and Non-Profit Management*, Addison Wesley/Open University, Wokingham, England.

Blair, T. (1994) *A New Approach*, Charity World, London.

British Standard The Quality Question BS EN ISO 9000, LGMB.

Bowman, C. and Asch, D. (1987) *Strategic Management*, Macmillan, London.

Bruce, I. (1992) *It's Time we Grew our own Managers'*, Charity, London.

Bruce, I. (ed.) (1993) *Charity Talks on Successful Development*, Volprof, City University Business School, London.

Bruce, I. and Leat, D. (1993) *Management for Tomorrow*, Volprof, City University Business School, London.

Bruce, I. and Raymer, A. (1992) *Managing and Staffing Britain's Largest Charities*, Volprof, City University Business School, London.

Bryson, J. M. (1988) *Strategic Planning for Public and Non-Profit Organisations*, Jossey-Bass, San Francisco.

Bryson, J. M. (1994) In *Preparing for the Future of Non-Profit Management*, Jossey-Bass, San Francisco.

Craig, J. C. and Grant, R. M. (1993) *Strategic Management*, Kogan Page, London.

Crosby, P. B. (1984) *Quality Without Tears*, McGraw-Hill, New York.

Drucker, P. F. (1990) *Managing the Non-Profit Organisation*, Harper Collins, New York.

Handy, C. (1988) *Understanding Voluntary Organisations*, Penguin, London.

Harrington, J. H. (1986) *The Improvement Process: How America's Leading Companies Improve Quality*, McGraw-Hill, New York.

Hartte, F. (1994) Performance Management – Where is it going? From *Competency Based Human Resource Management*, Hay Group, London.

Herman, R. (1994) *Preparing for the Future of Non-Profit Management*, Jossey-Bass, San Francisco.

Hinton, N. (1993) Planning for Growth in Charity Talks on Successful Development. In: *Charity Talks on Successful Development*, I. Bruce (ed.), Volprof, City University Business School, London.

Juran, J. M. and Gryna, F. M. (1993) *Quality Planning and Analysis*, McGraw-Hill, London.

Kearns, H. P., Krasmon, R. J. and Meyer, W. S. (1994) *Why Non-Profit Organisations are Ripe for Total Quality*, in *Nonprofit Management and Leadership*, Jossey-Bass, San Francisco.

Knight, B. (1993) *Centris Report*, Home Office, London.

Landry, C., Morley, D., Southwood, R. and Wright, P. (1985) *What a Way to Run a Railroad*, Camedia, London.

Leat, D. (1993) *Managing Across Sectors*, Volprof, City University Business School, London.

Manley, K. (1994) *Financial Management for Charities and Voluntary Organisations*, ICSA, London.

Marsden, D. and Richardson, R. (1991) *Does Performance Pay*

Motivate? A Study of Inland Revenue Staff, London School of Economics, London.

Mintzberg, H. (1994) *The Rise and Fall of Strategic Planning Business Policy in Action Pub. in Management Decision*, Prentice Hall, New York.

Oakland, J. S. (1989) *Total Quality Management*, Butterworth Heinemann, New York.

Ott, S. J. (1991) *Non-Profit Management and Leadership*, Jossey-Bass, San Francisco.

Øvretveit, J. (1994) 'Roads to recovery', *Health Service Journal*, London.

Peters, T. and Waterman, R. (1984) *In Search of Excellence*, Harper & Row, New York.

Peters, J. (1993) *Business Policy in Action in Management Decision*, MCB, London.

Pirsig, R. (1974) *Zen and the Art of Motorcycle Maintenance*, Bodley Head, London.

Prince Phillip (1994) *Arnold Goodman Lecture*, CAF, London.

Saint, D. (1994) *Strategic Planning – Buzzing or Boring in Voluntary Organisations Briefing*, Croner, Kingston-upon-Thames.

Saxon-Harrold, S. and Kendall, J. (eds) (1995) Dimensions of the Voluntary Sector, CAF, London.

Smith, R. (1994) *The Chronicle of Philanthropy*.

Spence, C. quoted in Dartington, T. (1994) *Mission Possible*, NCVO, London.

Steenberg, R. (1990) *Non-Profit Management and Leadership*, Jossey-Bass, San Francisco.

Stewart, V. (1990) *The David Solution*, Gower, London.

Stewart, J. and Walsh, K. (1989) *The Quality Question*, LGMB, Luton, England.

The British Quality Foundation (1995) *UK Quality Award Self-Assessment Guide*, The British Quality Foundation, London.

Unterman, I. and Davis, R. H. (1982) *The Strategy Gap in Not-for-Profits*, Harvard Business Review, Boston.

Valuing Management Development (1993) LGMB, Luton, England.

Waterman, I. and Davis, R. H. (1982) *The Strategy Gap is Not-for-Profit*, Harvard Business Review, Boston.

Weisbord, B. (1987) *The Non-Profit Economy*, Harvard University Press, Cambridge, MA.

Whitelaw, Viscount (1995) The 12th Arnold Goodman Charity Lecture, CAF, London.

Zeithaml, V. A., Parasuraman, A. and Berry, L. L. (1990) *Delivering Quality Service: Balancing Customer Perceptions and Expectations*, Free Press, New York.

Suggested further reading

Strategic planning

Barnard, H. and Walker, P. (1994) *Strategies for Success*, NCVO, London.

Brown, C. (1992) *Managing Change in Health and Social Care*, Pavillion, Brighton, England.

Egan, G. (1985) *Change agent skills in helping and Human Service Settings*, Brooks/Cole, Monterey, California.

Gawlinski, G. and Graessle, L. (1988) *Planning Together*, Bedford Square Press, London.

Gleave, R. (1992) *Business Planning in Health and Social Care*, Pavillion, Brighton, England.

Lowrie, A. (1994) *The complete guide to business and strategic planning for voluntary organisations*, Directory of Social Change, London.

Webb, S. (ed.) (1990) *Planning Strategy for Voluntary Organisations*, Industrial Society Press, London.

Quality

Astbury, R. (1993) *Quality Assurance in the Voluntary Sector*, NCVO, London.

Bone, D. and Griggs, R. (1989) *Quality at Work*, Kogan Page, London.

Care Sector Quality: A Training Manual (1994), Longman, Harlow, Essex.

Cassam, E. and Gupta, H. (1992) *Quality Assurance for Social Care Agencies*, Longman, Harlow, Essex.

Casson, S. and George, C. (1995) *Culture Change for Total Quality*, Pitman, London.

Catterick, P. (1992) *Total Quality – An Introduction to Quality Management in Social Housing*, Institute of Housing, London.

Chase, R. (ed.) (1992) *Service Excellence – the Best of 'Managing Service Quality'*, IFS Publications, Bedford, England.

Dickens, P. (1994) *Quality and Excellence in Human Services*, Wiley, West Sussex, England.

James, A. (May 1993) *Inside Quality Assurance*, Community Care Insert.

Kennedy, L. W. (1991) *Quality Management in the Non-profit World*, Jossey-Bass, San Francisco.

Lowrie, A. (undated) *Quality of Service*, NCVO/Directory of Social Change, London.

Martin, W. B. (1991) *Managing Quality Customer Service*, Kogan Page, London.

Oakland, J. S. (1993) *Total Quality Management*, Butterworth Heinemann, Oxford.

Pollitt *et al.* (1992) *Considering Quality: An Analytical Guide on Quality and Standards in Public Services*, Brunel University, London.

Stewart, J. and Walsh, K. (1991) *The Search for Quality*, Local Government Management Board, Luton, England.

BS EN ISO 9000 – The standard itself is published by the British Standards Institution BSI: Linford Wood, Milton Keynes MK14 6LE, Tel: (01908) 221166 or 220022. A set of free booklets on quality are available as part of the 'Managing in the 90's' programme from the Department of Trade and Industry, Tel: 0800 500 200.

Competencies/NVQs

Fletcher, S. (1991) *NVQs Standards and Competence: A Practical Guide for Managers and Trainers*, Kogan Page, London.

Fletcher, S. (1993) *Quality and Competence: Integrating Competence and Quality Initiatives*, Kogan Page, London.

Milrani, A., Dalzel, M. and Fitt, D. (eds.) (1992) *Competency Based Human Resource Management*, Hay Group/Kogan Page, London.

Weightman, J. (1994) *Competencies in Action*, Institute of Personnel and Development, London.

Investors in people

'Investors in People' Toolkits (1991) Employment Department, Sheffield.

'Investors in People' and Management Standards (1993) MCI, London.

Management development

Adirondack, S. (1992) *Just About Managing*, LVSC, London.

Baine, S., Coleman, N. and Hilditch, S. (1994) *Management Standards and the Voluntary Sector*, NCVO, London.

Batsleer, J., Cornforth, C. and Paton, R. (1991) *Issues in Voluntary and Non-profit Management*, Open University/Addison Wesley, Wokingham, England.

Bruce, I. and Leat, D. (1993) *Management for Tomorrow*, Volprof, London.

Croner's 'Management of Voluntary Organisations' (first published 1989 with regular updates) Croner, Kingston-upon-Thames, Surrey.

Drucker, P. F. (1990) *Managing the Non-profit Organisation*, Harper Collins, New York.

Going for better management (1988), Local Government Management Board, Luton, England.

Management Development Team (1994) *Voluntary Sector Use of the MCI Management Standards*, NCVO, London.

Metcalfe, B. A. (1990) *Identifying Management Potential: Techniques for Assessment*, Local Government Management Board, Luton, England.

Mumford, A. (1993) *Management Development, Strategies for Action* (2nd edn.), Institute of Personnel Management, London.

Paton, R. and Hooker, C. (undated) *Developing Managers in Voluntary Organisations – A Handbook*, Open University/Employment Department, Sheffield.

Proctor, J. (1991) *Using Competencies in Management Development*, NHS Training Directorate, Bristol.

Smith, L. (1993) *Valuing Management Development*, Local Government Management Board, Luton, England.

Stemp, P. (1988) *Are You Managing?*, Industrial Society Press, London.

Using Management Standards to Improve Organisational Effectiveness (undated), NHS Training Directorate, Bristol.

As well as the management standards themselves (in various formats), a wide range of materials are available from the Management Charter Initiations (MCI) on management standards and their use. They publish both a free directory of their own products and approved products from the agencies.
MCI
Russell Square House
10–12 Russell Square
London WC1B 5BZ
Tel: 0171 872 9000

Voluntary sector management (general)

An Introduction to Management in the Voluntary Sector, Compass Partnership.

Suggested further reading

Butler, R. and Wilson, D. (1990) *Managing Voluntary and Non-profit Organisations: Strategy and Structure*, Routledge, London.

Holloway, C. and Otto, S. (1985) *Getting Organised: A Handbook for Non-statutory Organisations*, Bedford Square Press/NCVO, London.

Hudson, M. (1995) *Managing Without Profit*, Penguin, London.

Index

Accessability, 31
Accountability, 4, 6, 31, 88
Accounting, 4
Accreditation, 95, 104, 112, 119, 144
Administration, 105
Advice guidance and counselling, 105
Advice-giving, 52
Advocacy, 34, 40, 45, 148
Age Concern England, 29
Aggressive and abusive behaviour, 106, 107, 108, 109
Aims, 22, 34, 44, 48, 51, 60, 62, 67, 68, 69, 73, 102, 112, 114, 115, 137, 139, 146
Ansoff, 19
Anti-discriminatory practice, 105
Appraisal, 10, 68, 71, 103, 104, 110, 118, 131, 134
Appropriateness, 31
Armstrong, M, 65, 66
Arnold Goodman Lecture, xi, 2
Attitude Surveys, 98
Autism, 30
Autonomy, 13

Barnardos, xii, 34
Barry Knight, xi
Belfast Improved Houses, 94
Bellah, 15
Benchmarking, 54, 103
Best practice, 41, 54
BHAGs, 44
Bias for action, 13
Blair, Tony, 2
Boston Consultancy Group, 42
Brainstorming, 146
British Quality Foundation, 99
Bruce and Leat, 10
Bruce and Raymer, xi, 10
Bruce, I, 5, 20, 120
Bryson, J, 23
BS EN ISO 9000, 8, 74–99, 145

Budgets, 24, 57, 114, 133, 146
Business plan, 22

Campaigning, 14, 26, 40, 45, 141, 148
Care–NVQs, 102, 105, 117
Care in the Community, 4
Cash flow projection, 58
Catering, 117
CCETSW, 118
Centris report, xi
Charitable status, 14
Charities Act, 4
Charities Aid Foundation (CAF), xi
Charity Commissioners, xi
Charles Handy, xii
Chief executives, 10, 20
Child Poverty Action Group, xii
Childcare and education, 105
Children, 45
Children Act, 5
Choice, 31
Citizens Charter, 32
Client customer focus, 31
CND, xii
Co-operation, 15, 144
Coaching, 67
Collaborating, 14
Collins and Parras, 44
Columbus, Christopher, 18
Commitment, 60, 66, 100, 113–116, 121, 129, 130, 140
Communicability, 61
Communication, 33, 105, 109, 139, 140
Community work, 105
Competencies, 1, 17, 66, 70, 102, 114–139
Competition, 15
Competitive, 20
Complaints, 33, 144
Confidentiality, 33, 105
Conflict, 127
Consensus, 61

169

Conservation, 29
Consultants, 56, 94
Consultation, 140
Contextualisation, 110, 130
Contingency plans, 21, 38, 39, 54, 58
Continuous improvement, 27, 34, 74, 86, 97, 98, 103, 122, 131, 136, 140, 145
Contract culture, 15
Contracting, 3, 4, 7
Corporate responsibility, 13
Councils for Voluntary Service, xii
Craig and Grant, 23
Criminal justice, 105
Crisis management, 19
Critical success factors, 22
Crosby, 75
Cultural venues, 105
Culture, 22, 24, 32, 136
Customer care, 13, 81, 98
Customer satisfaction, 8, 100

Deafblind people, 147
Delegation, 130
Develop teams, 126
Development plan, 21, 22
Direct marketing, 105
Disability, 30, 35
Disciplinary, 33, 127
Diversity, 34
Document control, 91
Donors, 21
Dreaming, 27
Drucker, P, 13, 28, 44, 51, 112

Easy to use complaints, 31
Education, 45
Effectiveness, 31, 114, 143
Efficiency, 6, 31, 144
Eisenhower, Dwight D, 21
Empowerment, 8, 13, 67, 98, 136
Environment, external, 1, 6, 7, 18, 24, 38, 129
Environmental conservation, 105
Environmental destruction, 26
Equal opportunities, 31, 32, 40
Equality, 105
Equity, 31, 143
Ethical value base, 12
European Union, 5
Evaluation, 8, 9, 25, 27, 36, 59, 78, 86, 103, 112, 114, 124–138, 145
Excellence, 15, 16, 31
Excellence indicators, 100
Excellence, the quest for, 137
External environment, 38

Fairness, 31
Family care and education, 105
Family support, 45
Feedback, 126, 139, 140
Finance, 55, 57, 58, 85, 137
Financial control, 10
Financial indicators, 49
Financial management, 9
Financial plan, 22
Firefighting, 19
Flat and flexible organisations, 13
Focus group, 27, 78
Force field analysis, 38
Funders, 8, 21, 26, 40, 57, 77, 79, 138, 141, 143, 144
Funding, 24, 51, 54, 116, 147
Fundraising, 47, 49, 54, 148

Gap analysis, 89
Goals, 9, 22, 27, 114, 122, 136
Grant Aid, 3
Grievance, 33, 127, 144

Handy, Charles, 7, 11,
Harrington, 77
Hartte, F, 65
Health and Safety, 33, 106, 144
Health care, 105
Help The Aged, 30
Herman, Robert, 15
Hierarchy, 12
High standards, 31
Hinton, N, xiii, 30
Homelessness, 79, 116, 141–144
Hostel, 81, 88
Housing, 105
Housing Associations, 3, 93, 94
Human resource strategy, 21, 56
Human resources, 55

Ideological fanaticism, 11, 12
Impact indictators, 22
Implementation, 24
Income generation, 9, 137
Independence and choice, 143
Induction, 10, 56, 117
Industrial Society, 103
Information, 128
Information and library services, 105
Initiative overload, 135
Inspection, 86, 91
Inter agency collaborations, 13
Intermediary bodies, xii
Internal customers, 84, 85
Investors in people, 1, 10, 102, 14–121, 135–139, 145

Involvement of all staff in decisions, 13
Issues impact analysis grid, 39

Job descriptions, 99, 110, 117, 131
Job evaluation, 131
Juran and Gryna, 75

Kearns *et al*, 8
Key results areas, 22

Landry *et al*, 7
Leadership, 12, 56, 99, 122
Lean staff, 13, 14,
Leat, Diana, 11, 13
Lifeboat Institution, xii
London Lighthouse, 20

Management charter initiative (MCI), 10, 120–129, 134, 145
Management development, 32, 122, 131–135
Management development methods, 133
Management standards, 122, 135
Management systems, 56
Managing finance, 123, 124, 125
Managing information, 123, 124, 125
Managing operations, 123
Managing people, 100, 123, 124, 125
Marketing, 90
Marsden and Richardson, 65
Measures of success, 22, 48, 50, 58, 60, 62, 137
Mencap, 30, 45
Mental health problems, 26
Mintzberg, Henry, 27
Mission, 7, 13, 14, 15, 18, 22, 24, 28–32, 34, 37, 41, 44, 46, 60, 62, 63, 98, 100, 112, 129, 141, 147
Moments of truth, 79, 81
Monitoring, 24, 58, 62, 63, 70, 106
Mutual support, 26

National Council for Vocational Qualifications 105
National management standards, 120, 139
National Trust, xii
National Vocational Qualifications (NVQs), 10, 105–119, 132, 135, 139
Natural Autistic Society, 30
NCVO, 122
Negotiating contracts, 9
NI Association of Mental Health, 29
NI Volunteer Development Agency, 30, 45

Non-executive imput at a strategic level, 13
Non-profit management and leadership, 7
Normalisation, 31

Oakland, 75
Objectives, 6, 14, 18, 21, 22, 24, 25, 51–73, 102, 112–115, 126, 128, 137, 144
One to one structured interviews, 27
Openness, 31
Operational plan, 22
Organisational development, 16, 133–138
Organisational development model, 137
Organisational model, 85
Ott, J Steven, 7
Outcomes, 6, 46, 48, 84, 128, 137
Outputs, 128, 137

Paddington Consultancy Partnership, 122
Pareto principle, 52
Participation, 144
Partners, 14
Partnerships, 6, 14, 21, 31, 37, 148
Pension, 56
People development, 31
People management, 100
Performance indicators, 22, 48, 137
Performance management, 1, 16, 64–73, 113, 135–139
Performance measures, 50
Performance related pay, 65, 66
Performance reviews, 68, 71
Person specifications, 99, 110, 128, 131
Personal effectiveness model, 128
Personnel, 85, 127, 128
Peters and Waterman, 13
Peters, T, 97
Philosophy, 22
Physical disability, 26
Plain english, 31
Plan of care, 108
Plans, 18
Playwork, 105
Policies, 22
Portfolio analysis, 41, 42
Portfolios for NVQs, 110, 132
Potteries Housing Association, 116
Premises, 40
Prevention, 8, 60, 86
Prince Philip, xi
Principles, 21, 22, 28, 31, 114

Privacy, 31
Private sector, 11, 14, 20
Procedures, 8, 87, 88, 100
Process, 100
Process model, 87
Productivity through people, 13
Professionalism, 12
Programmes, 18, 22
Projects, 22
Public relations, 41, 90, 105
Purchasing, 91
Purpose, 22

Quality, 7, 8, 10, 33, 34, 40, 41, 45, 113, 118
Quality action teams, 95
Quality assurance and management, 1, 9, 16, 17, 74–101, 135, 137, 139, 145
Quality assurance systems, 8
Quality auditors, 95
Quality audits, 91
Quality costs, 96
Quality culture, 98
Quality management, 8, 121
Quality people, 102–119
Quality policy, 95
Quality standards, 9, 58, 74, 89, 102, 143
Quality systems, 87
Quality teams, 8
Questionaires, 27

Raising income, 10
Recruitment, 1, 10, 56, 102, 103, 104, 112, 116, 119, 120, 124, 126, 128, 131, 139
Redress, 31, 144
Research, 40, 46
Residential home, 81, 117
Resources, 6, 21, 54, 55, 56, 62, 63, 100, 114, 123, 137, 143
Respect, 31
Responsiveness, 31
Retail, 105
Rogers, E, 60
Role clarification, 10

Saint, David, 19
Salary costs, 56
Save the Children, xiii, 29, 30
Schizophrenia, 26, 79
Scope, 35
Scrutiny report, 4

Self-help, xii
Senior management standards, 129, 130, 134
Senior managers personal competencies, 130
SENSE, 34, 45, 147
Sensory deprivation, 105
Sensory impaired people, 147
Service delivery, 26
Service life cycle, 42
Sexual abuse, 26
SHAW Homes, 117, 118, 119
Shelter, xii
Simon Community Northern Ireland, 141
Simple form, 13, 14
Simultaneous loose–tight properties, 13, 14
Single parents, xii
Skills, 6, 9, 10, 15
SMART, 51, 70
Smith, Richard, 15
Social Services, 3
SORP II, 4
Spastics Society, xii
Special needs housing, 105
Spence, Christopher, 20
Sport and recreation, 105
Staff, 21
Stakeholders, 7, 26, 27, 40, 41, 75, 77, 79, 130, 137
Standards, 4, 6, 8, 21, 22, 49, 63, 66, 67, 70, 100, 104, 136, 137
Staying close to the customer, 13
Steenberg, 65
Stewart and Walsh, 82
Stewart, V, 97
Sticking to the knitting, 13, 14
Strategic, 23
Strategic options, 25
Strategic planning, 9, 10, 14, 16, 18–63, 102, 114, 134, 135, 138, 140, 143, 146, 148
Strategic planning and management, 1, 7, 8, 16, 17, 18–63, 114, 121
Strategic pyramid, 33, 48, 53, 54, 59
Structures, 12, 56
Sub-objectives, 22
Success, 12
Succession planning, 10, 131
Supervision, 70
Supplier–Customer chain, 84
Survival, 25
SWOT analysis, 34, 38, 40, 42, 46, 62
Systems and procedures, 40

Target group, 25, 26
Targets, 22, 64, 66, 67, 70, 73, 114, 122
Teams, 25, 73, 99, 140
Teamwork, 13, 31, 98
Technology, 5, 40
The Princes Youth Business Trust, 29
Threats, 17, 18
Total quality management, 8, 67, 97, 99, 100, 119, 145
Training, 9, 10, 40, 56, 67, 85, 88, 89, 91, 92, 103, 104, 113, 119, 122, 133, 144, 146
Training and development, 1, 8, 9, 16, 32, 70, 105, 110, 112, 113, 114, 119, 132, 138, 140
Training needs, 104, 110–118
Trends, 129
Trustees, 6, 9, 21, 26

UK Quality Award, 99
Unemployment, 26
Unique selling points, 21

United response, 35
Unterman and Davis, 19

Value base, 105, 106
Value for money, 40
Value driven, 13
Values/principles, 6, 13, 14, 21, 22, 24, 28, 30–34, 41, 44, 46, 60, 63, 100, 105, 112, 141, 143, 146
Vision, 7, 18–28, 44, 98, 100, 114, 119, 136–140, 147
Voluneering, 45
Volunteers, 6, 10, 21

Weisbord, 5
Whitelaw, Viscount, 2
Worldwide Fund for Nature, 29

Young people, 2

Zeithaml *et al*, 78